Titles in the series

www.amazingstoriesbooks.com

LATE-BREAKING
AMAZING STORIES™

INSIDE THE WAR IN AFGHANISTAN

The hunt for al-Qaeda

by Sheila Enslev Johnston

PUBLISHED BY ALTITUDE PUBLISHING LTD.
1500 Railway Avenue, Canmore, Alberta T1W 1P6
www.amazingstoriesbooks.com
1-800-957-6888

In order to make this book as universal as possible, all currency
is shown in U.S. dollars.

Publisher	Stephen Hutchings
Associate Publisher	Kara Turner
Canadian Editor	Brendan Wild
U.S. Editor	Julian S. Martin
Layout & design	Bryan Pezzi

We acknowledge the financial support of the Government
of Canada through the Book Publishing Industry Development
Program (BPIDP) for our publishing activities.

ALTITUDE GREENTREE PROGRAM
Altitude Publishing will plant twice as many trees as were used
in the manufacturing of this product.

Cataloging in Publication Data
Enslev Johnston, Sheila
    Inside the war in Afghanistan / Sheila Enslev Johnston. -- Canadian ed.

(Late breaking amazing stories)
Includes bibliographical references.
ISBN 1-55265-309-9 (American mass market edition)
ISBN 1-55439-512-7 (Canadian mass market edition)

    1. Afghan War, 2001-. 2. Qaida (Organization). 3. Bin Laden, Osama, 1957-.
I. Title. II. Series.

| DS371.412.E57 2006 | 958.104'7 | C2006-901245-8 (Cdn) |
| DS371.412.E57 2006a | 958.104'7 | C2006-901244-X (U.S.) |

Printed and bound in Canada by Friesens
2 4 6 8 9 7 5 3 1

To my husband, Major Paul Johnston, who is currently in Afghanistan (2006) and also served in the mission to Afghanistan (2003).

Afghanistan

CONTENTS

Former Arizona Cardinal Patrick Tillman was killed in Afghanistan. He left a multimillion-dollar NFL contract to join the Army Rangers. The White House issued a statement that praised Tillman as "an inspiration both on and off the football field." For more on his story, see Chapter 1.

Members of the Canadian army's 12 Field Squadron 1 Combat Engineer Regiment take cover as they blast away a rock wall in May 2002. The soldiers were searching for Osama bin Laden's cave hideout in the Tora Bora region of Afghanistan. For more on the Tora Bora stronghold, see Chapter 5.

The basic equipment load for coalition forces.

Coyotes—light armored reconnaissance vehicles used in Afghanistan have the capability for both day and night operations.

The first day of elections in Afghanistan. Military forces were on heightened alert.

A B-2 Spirit stealth bomber near McGuire Airforce Base, New Jersey.

A B-52 drops a load of bombs. Air Force B-1 Lancers, B-2s, B-52 long-range bombers, and carrier-based strike aircraft have all been used in Afghanistan.

Afghan president Hamid Karzai photographed
in January 2006. See Chapter 6 for more
information on the president.

Lieutenant Colonel Mark Stammer (left), commander of U.S. forces in Afghanistan, meets with Governor Arman of Zabul province to discuss unsecured weapons caches. For more on Lt. Col. Mark Stammer's role in the rebuilding of Afghanistan, see page 141.

CHAPTER 1

An American Hero in Afghanistan

Bullets ricocheted off the stony ground around U.S. Army Ranger Corporal Patrick Tillman as he desperately rolled away and pulled himself into a sitting position. Frantically waving his arms, he shouted back to his comrades for fire support. It was dusk, and the Army Rangers' patrol in the mountainous Afghan terrain faced disaster. The other half of his platoon had been ambushed. Tillman and the two men with him had been firing at the next ridge, and now bullets poured back and forth in the fading light. Heavy machine-gun fire stitched up the rocky ground around their position. Where was the enemy? Whose fire was chewing up their position? The only thing clear to the men of 2nd Platoon was that they had to battle their way out of this ambush, secure all their men, and consolidate for the night before darkness fell.

It was April 22, 2004, and they were in the worst part of Afghanistan—the wild mountains bordering Pakistan, the very place where Osama bin Laden was believed to be hiding. The Black Sheep, as 2nd Platoon was known, was doing what Patrick Tillman had volunteered for: carrying the fight in the war against terrorism right into the enemy's lair. For months they had been searching up and down these mountains either in their Humvees or on long, arduous foot patrols. Occasionally they were ambushed. Occasionally they attacked suspected Taliban or al

Qaeda remnants. And occasionally they arrested suspected combatants. Mostly, though, they patrolled up and down the rugged mountains, never knowing what was around the next bend. It was hard work, but they were Rangers—the Army's elite light infantry soldiers.

Patrick Tillman was no ordinary volunteer and no ordinary Ranger. A huge, thickly muscled man with a cleft-chin and chiseled good looks, Tillman could have been a poster boy for U.S. Army Ranger recruiting. In fact, he was. He was an NFL professional football player who walked away from a multimillion-dollar contract with the Arizona Cardinals to instead wage war against terrorism. After 9/11, this deeply serious young man concluded that adopting this battle was the only thing for him to do. He quietly and discreetly made arrangements with his team for a leave of absence. He then volunteered—not just for the Army, but for the Rangers. He didn't want to spend his hitch safe and secure and out of the theater. He preferred to be at the front, taking the war to the terrorists themselves. Nothing less, he believed, would do. So it was that on April 22, he found himself on that bleak, craggy ridge in Afghanistan's mountainous hinterland, desperately fighting for his life.

All day long, things had gone badly for the Black Sheep. The unit of which they were a part— A Company of the 2nd Battalion, 75th Ranger Regiment—had been in the mountains along the Pakistani border for days. Two days earlier, one of their Humvees had broken down due to a problem with its fuel pump. They had laid up near the town of Khost, and late in the evening of April 21 a helicopter from the main U.S. base at nearby Bagram had flown in the necessary part. The helicopter had then evacuated their company commander, to attend a planning meeting for the next phase of their search and destroy mission. The platoon commander of the Black Sheep, a young lieutenant named David Uthlaut, remained in charge while the men attempted to repair the Humvee. They were unsuccessful, and the next morning at first light, Uthlaut decided to tow the disabled vehicle behind another Humvee and proceed toward their next objective. After a few hours of grinding up the winding and painfully steep mountain roads, the front end of the crippled Humvee buckled, bringing the entire convoy to a halt near the Afghan village of Margarah.

The young platoon commander radioed for backup support. He requested a rendezvous with one of the large, military cargo helicopters, so that it could heft the Humvee and transport it back to base. Uthlaut's request, however, proved unworkable. Instead, the Tactical Operations Center at the main base in Bagram insisted "further mission delays were unacceptable." The platoon was ordered to make its way forward to the final objective for the day—the small village of Manah—which lay farther up in the mountains beyond a particularly steep canyon.

Corporal Pat Tillman, along with the other men of Black Sheep, cobbled together a plan as required. "Improvise, adapt, overcome," the

U.S. Army likes to say. The platoon rented a local truck, known as a *jinga*, and hooked the disabled Humvee up behind it. Then they divided into two groups. One group would press on toward Manah, where they had been told to "get boots on the ground." The second group would tow and escort the lame Humvee out of the mountainous backcountry to the nearest highway, where it would be retrieved by mechanics from the U.S. camp at Khost. After depositing the broken Humvee, this group would join up with the others. They would all spend the night in Manah, which was considered to be a friendly village although it was surrounded by some of the wildest mountains in Afghanistan.

The two groups set off just after 6 p.m. After only a short while, the local Afghan driver of the *jinga* the platoon had hired to tow the Humvee to the highway protested that he couldn't manage the narrow, winding route they had chosen. After some consideration, the group decided to give up on delivering the Humvee and instead

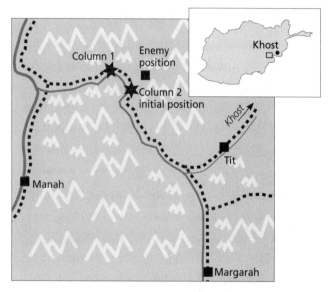

Sketch map showing the ambush
in which Pat Tillman was killed

set off to rejoin the rest of the platoon.

As dusk fell, the second group was ambushed. Fire stitched into their vehicles from
a distant ridge above the steep valley through
which they passed.

Determining that their fellow Black Sheep were in trouble, the first group halted. They dismounted to establish fire positions and to engage in yet another small, running gun battle with an isolated band of terrorists.

Patrick Tillman, who had been riding in the second Humvee of the platoon's lead group, was with two other men—a Ranger private and an Afghan soldier of the new pro-Western government based in Kabul. Under Tillman's direction, the three scrambled out of their Humvee and climbed a few yards up the steep, rocky ridgeline, where they found good fire positions near a large boulder. The other soldiers of the forward group, including platoon commander 1st Lieutenant Uthlaut, dismounted to find fire positions of their own. Together, they fired back at the ridgeline, where the enemy appeared to be.

At some point, Tillman volunteered to discard his heavy bulletproof vest and charge the distant ridgeline. With his history as a football player in the NFL, he was sure he could cover the distance. His offer, however, was refused, and the platoon continued to pursue more conventional strategy.

The second group, still under fire from the enemy, decided to break out of the ambush. Unable to distinguish what was going on based on the excited radio chatter, they gunned their engines and charged toward the lead group's location, hoping to break out of the ambush and link up with group one. As they came around the steep canyon's last bend, the second group's leader added his machine gun to the fire pouring forth from the group ahead. Seeing their commander firing, the other men of this unit followed standard practice and opened up, too. Two roof-mounted machine guns on the following-group's Humvees, pumped out their huge, .50-caliber rounds.

After several minutes of continuous firing into the glint of the setting sun, and men yelling and waving their arms to communicate amid the pandemonium, the shooting tapered off when the platoon commander and sergeants barked out the order to cease fire. The enemy had been driven off. However, the Afghan soldier lay dead, and Pat Tillman was dying. Tragically, in the chaos of this relatively insignificant skirmish, it was fire from the platoon's second group that killed these men.

In March 2006, the U.S. army announced an investigation into Pat Tillman's death. They maintain that the shooting was accidental, but concede that a criminal inquiry is warranted.

Corporal Tillman's death is but one dramatic and tragic episode in the overall story of the U.S.-led campaign against terrorism in Afghanistan, a campaign that has been overshadowed by the larger—but very different—war in Iraq. In fact, when compared to most of Afghanistan's long and unhappy history, the war in Afghanistan has been astonishingly and uniquely successful. There are many stories in this success that deserve to be told.

CHAPTER 2

Afghanistan's Tortuous History

fghanistan has always been a rugged and wild place where great armies and empires have come to grief. In spite of its remote nature, the country has seldom been left to mind its affairs unmolested.

Impassable mountains, particularly the famous Hindu Kush, lie to the north and south. Though dominated by mountainous terrain, the territory does include key valley passes.

The most important of these is a pass that has served as the land trade route between the East and West for centuries. The only practical path to join the Middle East to the Far East runs through this valley, which leads from ancient Persia (modern-day Iran), past Kandahar, through Kabul, and then eastward through the fabled Khyber Pass to India. Alexander the Great passed through the pass in 326 BC on his way to India. Later, so did Marco Polo. The silk trade between China and Europe relied on this route.

North of this vital trade link lies predominantly mountainous terrain, but in the area that forms what is now modern Afghanistan, more passable terrain does exist at its edges. This provides Afghanistan with a crucial "ring route" that forms a great circle around the rugged and near-impassable peaks. It is along the southern portion of this ring route that the ancient Silk Road ran through the area. The northern half of the ring route served as the invasion corridors down which Central Asians, in particular Genghis Khan, advanced toward the Middle East.

Ancient history

Alexander the Great was not alone in exploiting the Khyber to pursue his ambitions. He was followed in succeeding centuries by, amongst others, the Scythians, the Afghans and Mughals, the White Huns and Gokturks.

In AD 642, one of the most successful and influential of the invading armies arrived. Under the leadership of the Caliph—the successors to the prophet Mohammed—Arabs came to the territory invigorated by the new teachings of Islam. By the late 600s, they had converted the tribespeople of the area to Islam, and Islam remains the area's dominant religion to this day.

While Islam took root in Afghanistan, the Arab Caliphate did not. The Persians conquered the area in AD 998, and they were, in turn, displaced by Genghis Khan's Mongol invasion of 1219. Other invaders would follow. The result has been millennia of incessant warfare. The Afghan tribespeople probably viewed the consequences and appearance of this warfare as remarkably similar to another foreign army marching into the land seeking to subjugate the people. Afghans have cut their teeth on resisting such campaigns.

Ethnic makeup

The checkered history of this land has colored the ethnic makeup of the country. Afghanistan is a patchwork of peoples in which no single group forms a significant majority. Indeed, the population has never really formed a nation of peoples in the multicultural or "melting-pot" sense of the modern West. Instead, Afghanistan remains a culture deeply tribal in nature.

Among the patchwork of Afghanistan's eth-

APPROXIMATE ETHNIC BREAKDOWN IN AFGHANISTAN	
Pashtun	40 percent
Tajik	30 percent
Hazara	10 percent
Uzbek	10 percent
Other	10 percent

nic groups, two principal groups predominate. The first, and dominant, group is the Pashtuns. Numerically, the Pashtuns are the single largest group overall; they also form a geographic majority in a strip along the country's southern end. This area includes the critical Silk Road trade route of old, as well as the capital, Kabul. Ethnically, Pashtun tribes also spill over into the adjacent areas of what is now Pakistan. In fact, the term "Afghan" initially referred only to the Pashtun peoples living in Kabul and along the Silk Road trade route, not to all of what is now Afghanistan.

NATIVE LANGUAGES SPOKEN IN AFGHANISTAN
Dari (Afghan Persian) 50 percent (official language)
Pashtun 35 percent (official language)
Uzbek/Turkic 10 percent
Other 5 percent
Note: Multilingualism is common.

The northern half of Afghanistan, which includes the mountainous areas north of the old Silk Road, are dominated by branches of various Central Asian ethnic groups. The Tajiks are ethnic kinsmen to the Central Asians living in modern Tajikistan, while the Uzbeks are linked to modern Uzbekistanis. These two Central Asian peoples control the northern edge of the country and the ring route. The rugged and nearly impassable mountainous core of Afghanistan is home to the Hazara people.

Modern history

Afghanistan, as we are familiar with it today, first came into being in the mid-1700s. At that time, a local tribal leader of the Pashtuns consolidated power in the south and established himself as King Ahmad Shah Durrani, starting a dynasty based in Kabul. His family would dominate the politics of the country until the Mohammadzai clan took control in 1818.

The 19th century saw the beginning of a modern era in which great powers, in particular the British and the Russians, involved themselves in and fought for control over Afghanistan. Early in the century, sea travel rendered the Silk Road trade route far less crucial to foreign powers than it was in ancient times; nevertheless, Afghanistan still stood at a continental crossroads. Its geographic location caused it to bear the brunt of rival empires.

By the middle of the 19th century, the British had consolidated control of India. Their subsequent expansion brought them to the Khyber Pass and into contact with the Afghan kingdom. The result was the First Anglo-Afghan War fought from 1839 to 1842, in which the Afghans successfully deterred the British from expanding beyond what is modern Pakistan.

Under the czars, the Russians were simultaneously expanding from the opposite direction, and Afghanistan found itself caught up in the growth aspirations of these two great 19th-century empires. The Afghan kings, however, were able to effectively exploit the competing desires of expanding empires and use these opposing forces to their advantage: they variously played up to whichever side suited them.

During the Second Anglo-Afghan War (1878–1880), the Afghans were able to draw on support from the Russians that included western firearms critical in their struggle to fend off the British. This combat demonstrated once again what fierce warriors the mountain tribesmen of Afghanistan were, and the result was a series of treaties that guaranteed the independence of Afghanistan as a buffer state between the British and Russian empires.

In 1893, this arrangement was further refined when a British official, Lord Durand, visited the region to address and reconcile remaining grievances. The commission he led drew what came to be called "the Durand Line," which today still forms the border between Afghanistan and Pakistan. While this boundary reflected the balance of power at the time and outlined an independent state within which Afghan kings could develop, it nevertheless divided the Pashtun ethnic group between Afghanistan and what is now Pakistan. Inevitably, as often occurs when diplomats draw lines on maps to divide regions and ethnic groups, this split generated cross-border conflicts that continue to the present day.

At the beginning of the 20th century, Amir Abdul Rahman was the head of Afghanistan. He cultivated a pro-British foreign policy and in return, the British rewarded him with support that he deployed to quash tribal challenges to his rule. The Amir's grandson, Amanullah Khan, was not, however, clearly pro-British and when he assumed the crown in 1919, he declared full independence from British protection. This provoked skirmishes with British imperial forces in the area—the brief Third Anglo-Afghan War of 1919. The British appetite for warfare had been overindulged by World War I, and Britain was not interested in fighting to sustain imperial interests in distant Afghanistan. In August 1919, the British signed the Treaty of Rawalpindi and thus established Amanullah Khan's unchallenged reign in a fully independent Afghanistan.

Amanullah Khan was an educated modernizer determined to drag his kingdom into the 20th century and to make the nation a modern state. Despite his newly minted independence, Amanullah Khan had no better control over the country and its many tribal factions than did his predecessors. The many reforms he instituted and his secular approach—to say nothing of his habit of wearing Western-style suits—irritated the traditional tribal leadership across the country. Moreover, having fought and effectively expelled the British, he lacked the support his grandfather had drawn from them to keep dissenting and querulous tribal leaders in line. In 1929, Amanullah Khan was driven from Kabul and forced to abdicate, by an uprising led primarily by the Tajiks from the north.

The British seized upon this opportunity to reassert their influence: they sponsored one of Amanullah Khan's cousins, Nadir Shah, to assume the monarchy in October 1929. He, too, fell victim to Afghanistan's fractious politics and was assassinated within four years of assuming power. He was succeeded by his son, Muhammed Zahir Shah.

Assessments of Zahir Shah varied widely. He was considered by some to be sufficiently clever to placate all parties and thus run the country with few incidents and by others to be too lazy and uninterested in government to upset anyone and thereby provoke unrest. Regardless of the view one takes, under Zahir Shah's reign, Afghanistan enjoyed its longest sustained period of peace—from his coronation in 1933 to the coup that toppled him from power in 1973. During these 40 years, little was done to modernize the country, even as the modern, post-war world developed all around it and the countries on Afghanistan's borders—India and Pakistan—were achieving independence.

Coups and revolts

Ironically, after the assassination of Zahir Shah's uncle before him—which resulted in response to Amanullah Khan's desire to modernize and Westernize the country—it was likely frustration over the lack of modernization that prompted the overthrow of Zahir Shah. Sardar Muhammed Daoud led the coup in July 1973. Daoud, already prime minister (and the king's cousin), abolished the monarchy, assumed the positions of president and prime minister, and announced grand plans for the modernization of the country. Daoud's efforts to reform and modernize failed to satisfy the new urban elite, who were impatient for change, while displeasing traditional tribal groups. Moreover, his government lacked the legitimacy that the old monarchy had garnered in the eyes of many Afghans. Having shown the way to violent regime change, Daoud's methods were used against him and he was toppled in 1978 by an even more violent coup than the one he, himself, had instigated. This was known as the Saur Revolt.

Extremist modernizers—many of whom

held Marxist beliefs that were common in developing nations at that time—led the Saur Revolt. Directed by Nur Muhammed Taraki, the coup established what the new regime called the "Revolutionary Council" to rule the country. By this time, however, violence was so thoroughly established as the mechanism of political succession in Afghanistan that in fewer than 18 months Taraki, too, was ousted by a yet more ardent Marxist, Hafizullah Amin.

It is uncertain how many Afghans were killed during the power struggles that raged in the 1970s. The majority of the populace and the country as a whole was not directly affected. Nevertheless, several thousand citizens were killed in and around Kabul, and governmental stability and law and order throughout the land deteriorated, as the central government suffered repeated coups. Afghanistan was set on its descent into the chaos that typified its political process for a further quarter of a century.

How the Soviets came to invade Afghanistan

The 1979 Soviet invasion of Afghanistan remained a contentious event. It would eventually become clear that the fighting that ensued within the tiny country played a key role in the eventual collapse of the Soviet empire.

Of course, this was not what the Soviets had in mind when they occupied Afghanistan. Why the Soviets chose to invade and to what extent Hafizullah Amin "invited" Soviet intervention has been much debated over the years. At the time, most Western commentators saw the Soviet invasion as a move on the Cold War chessboard, one aimed to expand Soviet influence into Central Asia and, some speculated, to secure a warm-water port on the Indian Ocean.

In fact, with the benefit of hindsight and access to the former-Soviet archives, it seems clear that the Soviets were not motivated by such grand plans. Hafizullah Amin, struggling with tribal revolts, almost certainly invited the Soviet presence to prop up his regime. He would have likely fallen from power had he not done so, and as a Marxist-minded modernizer, it followed that he turn to the Soviet Union and not the West for support. For their part, the Soviets saw a friendly, pro-Marxist regime teetering on the brink of collapse, in a region where there was substantial concern about instability. Furthermore, the conventional Soviet response to such volatility was rapid invasion—as was executed in Hungary and Czechoslovakia in the 1950s and 1960s respectively. Doubtless, the Soviets expected the incursion to be quick and simple: it would enable them, in relatively short order, to install a new regime that would successfully modernize the country and install a stable, pro-Soviet government. The Soviets were not the first empire to harbor such delusions.

If Hafizullah Amin did invite the Soviet troops to invade, it was the most unfortunate decision of his brief government and one he would pay for with his life. The Soviets appear to have thought that while they needed a pro-Marxist government in Afghanistan, Hafizullah Amin was more an impediment than an asset in this regard. In December 1979, Soviet officers already established in Afghanistan as military advisors began planning and reconnaissance for a full-fledged Soviet invasion. On December 22, these Soviet advisors informed the Afghan government it was necessary to bring the majority of their tanks and other Soviet-supplied heavy equipment to Kabul for maintenance. It was, after all, the winter season.

With the bulk of the Afghan army's forces thus out of commission, Soviet advisors cut communication links between Kabul and the periphery of the country. Soviet airborne troops began streaming into the country from the neighboring Soviet republics of Tajikistan and Uzbekistan. At the head of these troops, dressed in Afghan uniforms, were Soviet Special Forces agents with the KGB. These Special Forces were airlifted into Kabul. They moved directly to the

THE TAJBEG AND DARUL-AMAN PALACES

The Tajbeg Palace, built in the 1920s, served as the official residence of the Afghan king and, after the 1973 Daoud coup, the country's president. It was here that President Hafizullah Amin holed up during the Soviet invasion of 1979 and was subsequently killed by Soviet Special Forces troops. During the Soviet occupation, it served as Soviet headquarters.

The Darul-Aman Palace, also built in the 1920s, was originally intended to house the national parliament. It is the larger and more famous of the two "palaces." It sits atop an imposing hill on the southwestern outskirts of Kabul. It was heavily damaged during the Afghan civil wars after the Soviets' withdrawal, but it is now scheduled for reconstruction and renovation by a German firm so that it can once again house the Afghan parliament.

Tajbeg Palace, where Hafizullah Amin had barricaded himself in. The Russians stormed the palace and killed Hafizullah Amin and several of his close advisors with a hail of submachine-gun fire. In his place, the Soviets installed Babrak Karmal, a lawyer and long-time member of the communist Peoples Democratic Party of Afghanistan (PDPA).

The new Soviet-installed regime proved incapable of controlling the inhabitants of the countryside beyond Kabul. As a Soviet puppet, Karmal had no legitimacy in the eyes of Afghanistan's tribal groups. The populace was even more antagonistic toward his regime than they had been with Hafizullah Amin—or with any of the preceding regimes as far back as Daoud. Confronted with the assassination of their president and offended by the high-handed treatment they received at the hands of the Soviet-installed government, morale in the Afghan army collapsed. Thousands of soldiers deserted and made their way back to their home tribal groups. By the summer of 1980, the only effective military force that remained in support of the Karmal regime in Kabul was the Soviet Army.

The Soviets now found themselves in a position like that of so many imperial forces before—isolated in the major towns and surrounded by Afghan tribes in full revolt. The ranks of those tribal fighters were now flush with soldiers who had deserted the Afghan army, and they initiated a long guerrilla war against the Soviets.

This was the early 1980s—the final period of Soviet–American Cold War tension and conflict. Ronald Reagan had just been elected president on a strong anti-Soviet platform, and the United States began to provide extensive support to the Afghan tribal group rebels fighting the Soviets. Also crucial in providing aid was Pakistan, which maintained close ties with their fellow ethnic Pashtuns and a strong interest in a non-Soviet Pakistan.

The rise of the mujahideen

Deeply conservative, Muslim traditionalists proved to be the critical constituent in the long war against the Soviets. They were crucial in sustaining anti-Soviet resistance and drew their strength from roots embedded in traditional tribal groups. Much of their antipathy towards the Soviets was grounded in the fact that the

Communists were avowed atheists—tribal elders viewed them as godless heretics.

Just as political agitation—much of it leftist—was common in western universities in the 1960s, the 1970s saw similar pervasive agitation throughout the universities of the Muslim world, including those in Pakistan and Afghanistan. Nur Muhammad Taraki, Hafizullah Amin, and Babrak Karmal had all been active in student politics as Marxists and Communists during that decade. Unlike in the West, however, where student protests were largely secular, protests in most of the Muslim third world was decidedly spiritual in nature.

A budding Islamic movement was building in the Muslim world. Fed up with what they saw as indifferent and insensitive domination by the non-Muslim west, the response was a school of thought that preached a return to Islamic purity and fierce independence from the West. The Islamic movement was inspired in great part by the theories of Hassan al Banna, an Egyptian political thinker of the 1920s who founded the Muslim Brotherhood. He argued for a return to Islamic virtues as a counterforce to the social injustice he saw simmering among the Egyptian poor. By the 1970s, al Banna's ideology had merged, to some extent, with other social and political movements of the time and fueled a surging interest in Islamic fundamentalism.

The anti-Soviet war in Afghanistan brought these opposing forces to a head. The guerrilla soldiers were known as *mujahideen*, and they drew their ranks from the long-established, traditional Muslim tribal constituency in the countryside and more contemporary Islamic fundamentalism in the cities. Combined, these forces proved formidable and they denied the Soviets the opportunity to secure control of the country.

One of the spiritual leaders of this religious resistance movement was Burhanuddin Rabbani. Prior to chaos and political instability resulting from the string of coups and counter-coups in the late 1970s, Rabbani was a Muslim scholar

at Kabul University. He was also an active political leader in the new Islamic movement. His
charisma and the ideals he advocated drew
many of Afghanistan's brightest young minds to
him. Among them were Gulbuddin Hekmatyar,
a university student in the engineering faculty,
and Ahmed Massoud, also an engineering student and the son of an Afghan army officer.

When the Soviets invaded, these three men
went to the hills to fight with the mujahideen.
Rabbani served in the role of a spiritual leader
among the fractious tribes. Massoud, following in his father's footsteps, became a respected
guerrilla military commander. Hekmatyar, who
in his youth was a member of the communist
PDPA before he turned to Islamic fundamentalism, became a factional leader with close ties to
supporters in Pakistan.

The Afghan resistance attracted widespread international backing. Under President
Reagan, the United States provided extensive
support to the various units of the mujahideen.

In particular, it advanced portable, heat-seeking antiaircraft missiles, which proved highly effective against the helicopters used extensively by the Soviets.

Predictably, support for the Afghan resistance came from the Muslim world as well. In addition to cash donations by many Muslim governments—in particular the oil-rich Middle Eastern sheikdoms—many young Muslim men, inspired by the spirit and objectives of the Islamic movement, traveled to Afghanistan to fight alongside the mujahideen. One of those young men was Osama bin Laden, a middle son from a large and wealthy Saudi family who was looking for a cause and, very likely, a way to prove himself.

The Soviets meet with defeat

The combined resources of the traditional tribal forces in the countryside, the new Muslim thinkers in the cities, and the forces contributed by foreigners, such as the Americans and Saudis, proved too much for the Soviets.

The 1980s brought an increasingly vicious guerrilla war to bear in Afghanistan, against which the Soviets slowly but surely lost ground. In 1986, Soviet power had deteriorated to such an extent that Karmal's position as the Soviet puppet-leader of the nation was tenuous. Then Karmal's head of secret police, Muhammad Najibullah, seized power and Karmal was forced to flee to Moscow. Najib, as Najibullah was known, held power for the duration of the war by employing increasingly brutal methods of political repression.

At the end of the decade, Soviet fighting forces were spent. Soviet president Mikhail Gorbachev was confronted by increasing demands for political and social reform in Eastern Europe and at home, and he decided to withdraw Soviet troops from a draining and increasingly unpopular war. On February 15, 1989, the final Soviet soldiers departed Afghanistan and retreated homeward by the same highway into Tajikistan along which so many of the original

Soviet forces had entered the country a full 10 years earlier.

When the Soviets departed, Najibullah remained president of Afghanistan. The mujahideen regarded him as a Soviet-installed puppet, and the coalition of resistant forces continued its fight against the Najibullah regime. These fighters battled on despite the loss of U.S. support for the mujahideen cause, which followed on the heels of the Soviets' departure. Support gleaned from Islamic cohorts, such as Osama bin Laden, became all the more important to resistance fighters and those who sought to establish political power.

Following the Soviet withdrawal, three years of civil war ensued between rival Afghan factions: the mujahideen, with its stronghold in the countryside, and the Kabul-based regime of Najib. Without Soviet support, Najibullah fought a losing battle, and in April 1992, the mujahideen triumphantly entered Kabul and declared Afghanistan an Islamic state. Najib fled from

Tajbeg Palace and took sanctuary in the United Nations compound in Kabul.

Scholar and spiritual leader Burhanuddin Rabbani came down from the mountains and was proclaimed the first president of this new Islamic state. Massoud was established as Rabbani's defense minister; Hekmatyar was appointed prime minister. However, the mujahideen remained as chaotic and conflict-ridden in government as they had been as guerrillas.

Almost immediately, a power struggle occurred and factions divided into two camps. On one side was the official government of Rabbani, with Massoud as military commander of the tribal militia forces. Opposing them was Hekmatyar, who commanded a considerable mujahideen force of his own. He refused to join the government despite having been appointed prime minister; instead, he and his forces remained in the hills surrounding Kabul and shelled the city with artillery. Most of the physical damage to Kabul, including the devastation

of the Darul-Aman Palace, dates from this conflict—caused, ironically, not during hostilities
with the Soviets but by Hekmatyar's forces.

The Taliban come to power

Chronic infighting within the Rabbani government fatally weakened its power and mandate
to govern. In the midst of the civil war that en-
gulfed the regime after the Soviet withdrawal, a
new group emerged: the Taliban.

The Taliban was one manifestation of the
resurgence of Islamic puritanism that began to
build in the Muslim world in the last decades
of the 20th century. *Talib* (the plural is *taliban*)
means "student"—in particular, a student en-
rolled in an Islamic school. Beginning near the
southern city of Kandahar, a religious movement
developed in the mid-1990s that stressed the fundamentalist interpretation of Islam as the cure
for the chronic ills that wracked Afghanistan.

The spiritual leader of the movement was
Mullah Omar, previously a village mullah from

the area. Virtually nothing is known about his background except that he fought with the mujahideen in the anti-Soviet war and that he lost an eye in the conflict. According to Taliban legend, he founded the movement after learning that a handful of lawless, violent Afghan mujahideen had kidnapped a number of pious Muslim women, taken them to their encampment where they held them captive, and raped them. Mullah Omar and a number of his students armed themselves and rescued the women. The story has likely grown in the telling. What is known is that by the mid-1990s, the endless civil war had produced considerable and widespread suffering that grew out of the loose soil of chaos. It is also true that in their own albeit puritanical way, the Taliban brought order to the areas they captured.

The Taliban insurrection blossomed and surged forth from its base in Kandahar, and in 1996, four years after the departure of Soviet forces, it captured Kabul. Rabbani fled north to the town of Faizabad, where he established the headquarters of what would later become the Northern Alliance. Massoud escaped with him and became the Northern Alliance's military commander. Hekmatyar fled to Iran. Najib, who remained concealed in the UN's Kabul compound, found the Taliban far less adherent to the rules of international convention than was Rabbani's government: the Taliban stormed the UN compound, seized Najib, and summarily executed him. They strung up his body in downtown Kabul for all to see.

For the next five years, the Taliban and Northern Alliance continued to fight a variation of the civil war that had begun, in its most recent incarnation, 23 years earlier. The Taliban benefited from the generous support supplied by the Pakistanis and by Islamic groups such as bin Laden's al-Qaeda. It benefited, also, from a certain tolerance manifested by the United States and other western governments, who either acknowledged no differences between

the various Afghan factions or who perceived
the Taliban to be a force that might bring order to bear on a persistently fractious, violent,
and unruly country at last. The result was a
growing, grinding Taliban supremacy over the
slowly shrinking forces of the Northern Alliance.

CHAPTER 3

Osama bin Laden and al-Qaeda

I t is not known definitively when Osama bin Laden, now the most famous of the foreign volunteers, first arrived in Afghanistan to fight the Soviets. However, he was certainly there within a year or two of the 1979 invasion. At the time, bin Laden had recently graduated from university and faced the prospect of beginning lifelong service in the family business—a business in which he, as a middle son, could never hope to inherit leadership. Perhaps it was to make a name for himself or to find adventure, or maybe it was some greater spiritual cause to counter his dissolute younger days in Beirut that spurred him to set out as a mujahideen in Afghanistan.

Whatever his initial motives, he found his niche in Afghanistan: by the early 1980s, bin Laden was actively organizing funding and support for various mujahideen groups. It is less clear whether he took an active role as a fighter on the battlefield. The lack of mythology illuminating his personal role in combat in Afghanistan strongly suggests this was not the task he set for himself. He did, however, provide the mujahideen with invaluable bankrolling for its cause and to organize support.

When the Soviets withdrew in 1989, bin Laden returned home to Saudi Arabia, where he met with a hero's welcome from family and friends. He appears to have relaxed during this time, basking in the glow of his success abroad,

OSAMA BIN LADEN BIOGRAPHY

Osama bin Laden was born in Riyadh, Saudi Arabia, to Mohammed Awad bin Laden, a wealthy business-man in the construction industry with close ties to the Saudi royal family. It is not clearly known how many children Mohammed Awad bin Laden fathered, but the number is generally agreed to be 52. Osama bin Laden came in the middle of this brood and is, by various accounts, estimated to be the 17th son.

Osama bin Laden was raised a devout Sunni Muslim. He earned a degree in civil engineering in 1979 from King Abdul Aziz University in Jeddah. In 1974, at the age of 17, bin Laden married his first wife, Najwa Gha-nem. Since then he has married four more women and has divorced at least one. He has fathered 24 children, perhaps more. He is a tall man—6 feet 4 inches—but he is spare, weighing only 160 pounds. He has an ol-ive complexion, is left-handed, and usually walks with a cane. He is soft-spoken and mild mannered, rather than fiery. Despite his reputation and rhetoric, he is said to be charming, polite, and respectful.

and then taken up some minor duties in the family business.

In 1990, the First Gulf War broke out. Bin Laden was immediately electrified by the conflict: he proposed to the Saudi government that he lead another mujahideen campaign (as he had done in Afghanistan) but this time directed against Saddam Hussein. Ties that the bin Laden family had with the Saudi royal family would ensure that Osama bin Laden had the opportunity to pitch his scheme personally to senior government officials. While those officials praised his enthusiasm, they declined his offer and ignored his advice. Instead, the Saudis invited a huge "infidel army"—the Americans—into their kingdom to pitch Hussein's troops out of Kuwait by force.

Osama bin Laden was outraged. His anger and indignation was further enflamed when significant contingents of U.S. forces remained in Saudi Arabia after the war. He became outspokenly anti-American and ever more anti-Western and extremist in his rhetoric. In 1992, confronting increasingly antagonistic relations with government authorities because of his views, he departed Saudi Arabia. At first, he returned to Afghanistan where he sought to mediate the strained relations between the now-feuding Rabbani and Hekmatyar factions, but he was entirely without success.

Bin Laden then settled in the Sudan, where the Islamic anti-Western government was sympathetic to his views. There he began to build the current structure of al-Qaeda—including camps in both Sudan and Afghanistan—and develop his jihadist crusade against the West.

By 1996, although not yet a household name in the West, Osama bin Laden was well

JIHAD

Jihad—an Arabic word in the sacred language of Islam—means "struggle" or "crusade." It has become a contentious term. The Prophet Mohammed used the expression when he declared jihad was the sacred duty of all Muslims. However, many argue that a proper reading of the *Koran* makes it clear Mohammed meant this in a spiritual sense: an inner struggle by all of the faithful to overcome their own sinfulness and weaknesses. Others—bin Laden and his followers in particular—use the term in an explicitly militant sense to mean holy war against those they perceive to be the enemies of Islam.

known for masterminding several anti-Western terrorist attacks. In response to these attacks, the United States brought enormous pressure to bear on the Sudanese government to expel him. That year they did, and bin Laden moved to Afghanistan, where he allied himself with the now ascendant Taliban. He established a network of at least a dozen training camps. It was from Afghanistan that bin Laden planned and directed his most famous terrorist attacks, including the 1998 embassy bombings in Nairobi, Kenya, and Dar es Salaam, Tanzania; the 2000 attack against the USS *Cole* in Yemen; and, most infamous of all, the September 11, 2001, hijacked airline attacks on New York and Washington, D.C.

Osama bin Laden's position within the extended bin Laden family has long been unclear. It is known, however, that his immensely wealthy family publicly disowned him in 1994, shortly before the Saudi Arabian government revoked his citizenship. Osama bin Laden attended the wedding of one of his sons in January 2001, but since 9/11, he is believed to have had contact with his mother on only one occasion.

* * *

Terrorism is not a novel invention, but what has been referred to as *world terrorism* in the wake of 9/11 is indeed new. And it is almost literally the creation of one man: Osama bin Laden.

What might be called "traditional" or conventional terrorism has been waged for almost as long as humans have occupied Earth. Contemporary anthropologists' studies of Stone Age cultures have confirmed that tribal warriors would periodically raid other tribes' villages with the specific objective of terrorizing their enemies. Even insurgents motivated by religion are hardly new. Roman legions, for example, spent much of their time in Judea (modern Israel) pursuing fighters of various sects that opposed Roman rule and who spread messianic claims about a divine mission. In contemporary contexts, movements such as Hamas and

Hezbollah have become fixtures of Middle Eastern strategic politics.

But all such terrorist movements were similar in that they tended to have quite specific, often territorial, claims. For all their talk about revolutions, what most terrorist organizations want is to become fairly conventional governments. For instance, Hamas and Hezbollah want to establish a Muslim, ethnically Arabic government on land that is now the territory of Israel. The IRA wants to establish a majority Catholic, Irish nationalist government in the territory of Northern Ireland. Around the world, from Basques in northern Spain to Tamils in Sri Lanka, most terrorist movements cherish very specific territorial objectives of this sort. Their use of terror as a weapon is calculated to force political concessions from the respective governments they oppose.

It is worth noting that because conventional terrorist groups commonly have specific objectives, such groups can be negotiated with, at least in theory and from the perspective of western nations not targeted by terrorists.

This is why terrorism was understood, until recently, to be a marginal threat to western societies, except, perhaps, for those unlucky enough to find themselves on the territory coveted by a specific terrorist movement, such as Northern Ireland in Great Britain and the Basque region of Spain. The United States, however, did not fit into this category and, with the exception of parts of Great Britain, neither did any major western country.

But al-Qaeda is fundamentally a different kind of terrorist organization. For example, while al-Qaeda has an evolving list of demands, some of which are in a sense territorial, these demands do not lie at the organization's core. For instance, one of al-Qaeda's substantive and most repeated initial demands was that U.S. military forces vacate the "sacred" territory of Saudi Arabia. New U.S. basing arrangements made this a reality in 2003: while some liaison, training, and support coordination personnel remain as individuals, there are now no U.S. military forces or combat units stationed in the Saudi kingdom. This fact, however, has not changed al-Qaeda's hostile attitude toward the United States. In fact, this development passed completely without comment from al-Qaeda spokesmen.

Al-Qaeda does not seek specific demands that can be negotiated or achieved with any given policy measure. Instead, it is motivated by a fundamentalist religious vision of the world and believes it has a comprehensive, "higher" mission. In essence, it is probably the practices and mores of a modern, technological, and free democratic society with which al-Qaeda is at war; al-Qaeda makes the United States its primary target because the United States is the greatest symbol and leading agent of modernity in the world today. To this end, al-Qaeda is prepared and motivated to cross oceans to strike the United States at home.

No other terrorist group has done this be-

fore. Only two successful foreign terrorist attacks have been launched in the United States,
and both were the work of al-Qaeda: the World
Trade Center bombing in 1993 and the subsequent 9/11 attacks on the World Trade Center
and the Pentagon. Al-Qaeda understands itself
as engaged in jihad—a global crusade motivated by fundamentalist Islam. Rahter than
territory objectives, it seeks a new order for
Muslims everywhere that is as much spiritual
as governmental.

This is why al-Qaeda represents such an
unpredictable and elusive danger. And while
the organization draws upon widespread social
conflicts in the Muslim world, it is almost solely
the creation of Osama bin Laden.

Steps in the al-Qaeda plot:
Ahmed Massoud

The first blow of al-Qaeda's heinous plan to hi-
jack aircraft in the United States and crash them
into high-profile New York and Washington, D.C.

targets was struck not on September 11, 2001, but two days earlier and half a world away in Afghanistan. On September 9, two Arab journalists were admitted access to Ahmed Massoud, military commander of the Northern Alliance, for an interview. Their passports identified them as Belgian citizens, originally from Morocco, and they claimed to be making a documentary for Aljazeera, the Arabic equivalent to CNN. These television journalists arrived laden with the bulky camera and sound equipment of their profession, apparently ready to conduct their interview with a willing Massoud.

Ahmed Massoud knew it was critical that he attract international attention to and support for his cause, particularly from the Muslim world that had supported the long insurgency against the Soviet occupation. On that fateful day, then, he agreed to meet with the journalists to spread his message. They met in a small, bare room located in one of the mud-brick houses that constituted the simple headquarters of the

Northern Alliance command.

At first, none in Massoud's entourage suspected that anything was awry. Then Masood Khalili, the Northern Alliance ambassador to India who happened to be present, noticed what he called "a nasty smile" on the cameraman's face. The two Arabic television journalists were, in fact, suicide bombers sent to assassinate Massoud. Powerful explosives were hidden within the conventional, bulky battery-packs and within the camera itself. The cameraman detonated both explosives once they were gathered in the interview room with Massoud. The explosion killed most of those present, including the two assassins. Massoud, although not killed instantly, died later that same day. His death was not announced to the public for some weeks.

The assassination was unquestionably the work of al-Qaeda. A copy of the written questions presented to Massoud's staff by the sham journalists was found on the hard-drive of a computer captured at an al-Qaeda camp after the Taliban's fall. The two assassins were later discovered to be Tunisian, traveling on stolen passports. The television camera they carried had been reported stolen by a tele-journalist in southern France a few months earlier.

No real doubt existed about who would want Ahmed Massoud dead. The terrorist attacks that struck the northeastern United States two days later indicated why bin Laden would want Massoud obliterated when he was. Al-Qaeda would have predicted a significant U.S. military reaction against their audacious hijacking attacks. Bin Laden also knew that the primary beneficiary of such retaliatory attacks on al-Qaeda and its Taliban allies would be the Northern Alliance, since the Northern Alliance, not the Taliban, was the real heir to the old U.S. alliance from the days of the mujahideen struggle against the Soviets. Inevitably, any U.S. retaliation would include support for the Northern Alliance.

How better to blunt the effectiveness of the Northern Alliance in such circumstances than to eliminate its best military commander on the eve of the attacks? Massoud was a brilliant military tactician. In fact, the Lion of the Panshir, as he was known, was the most senior tactician of the Northern Alliance. But he was also a master strategist, a keen statesman, and a charismatic leader who could rally the Northern Alliance forces and lead them against the Taliban in a new campaign capitalizing on U.S. support. And bin Laden knew it.

It is almost certain, however, that bin Laden did not correctly anticipate the scale of the U.S. reprisals that were to come. President Bill Clinton had ordered only individual cruise missile strikes in retaliation for previous al-Qaeda attacks. Bin Laden likely projected more of the same, though perhaps with heavier air strikes this time and maybe with increased support to the Northern Alliance. A weakened Northern Alliance would benefit al-Qaeda efforts. In bin Laden's calculation, the assassination of Massoud prior to the al-Qaeda attacks on U.S. soil would serve to limit the consequences for al-Qaeda and safeguard, to some extent, their position in Afghanistan.

Osama bin Laden was terribly mistaken.

CHAPTER 4

Operation Enduring Freedom: Toppling the Taliban

The B-52s circled high above, appearing deceptively peaceful as they made what looked to be lazy, gentle turns. The effect on the ground, however, was spectacular. Serenely safe at their high altitude, the B-52s were dropping joint direct attack munitions (JDAMs), pounding antiaircraft gun placements around the airfield on Kabul's northern edge. The giant U.S. aircraft and the bombs they dropped were weirdly silent, but the explosions that burst ferociously—seemingly from nowhere and precisely on the Taliban gun positions—rocked the land. Shortly thereafter, the rumblings of further explosions were heard in the distance, and the power in the city was abruptly extinguished.

It was Sunday, October 7—less than a month after the September 11 terrorist attacks in the

JOINT DIRECT ATTACK MUNITIONS

JDAMs are among the most modern "smart bombs," or what the military calls precision guided munitions (PGMs). Each bomb has a built-in Global Positioning System receiver that enables the bomb to calculate its position with tremendous accuracy. The bomb then guides itself to the target coordinates with equal accuracy. This gives modern PGMs two key advantages over traditional laser-guided bombs. First, they are reliable in all kinds of weather, and second—because the bombs are self-contained—the dropping aircraft do not require special fittings, such as the old-style laser designators. In Afghanistan, the venerable 1950s-era B-52s were used to drop great quantities of JDAMs.

United States—and Operation Enduring Freedom had begun. U.S. aircraft and cruise missiles, launched by the U.S. and British navies, initiated a carefully choreographed series of air strikes designed to hit the terrorists harboring in Afghanistan and to ultimately topple the Taliban regime that had granted them refuge.

For the first few days, the bombing focused on the most prominent al-Qaeda training camps and the Taliban's air defense capabilities. After more than 20 years of continuous warfare in Afghanistan, the Taliban was impoverished and effectively isolated from the rest of the world. Consequently, the Taliban had few radar installations, limited antiaircraft guns, and only a handful of transport aircraft and helicopters. It possessed no working antiaircraft missiles.

The first step in any air campaign, however, is to destroy any existing capabilities—meager though they may be—so that American airpower could confidently shift its focus to the al-Qaeda militia and the Taliban themselves, with-

THE B-52 AND B-2 BOMBERS

The B-52 is an old airplane; development began in 1946 and the first test flight was completed in 1952. The B-52s now in service have been overhauled many times. They still serve a useful function because they are so large and can haul very heavy loads for long-range missions.

The B-2 is a smaller, more modern airplane. A stealth bomber, it is designed to be invisible to enemy radar. B-2s carry modern smart bombs, and with their enormous range they are capable of operating around the world from bases in the continental United States.

out interference from the ground.

The Taliban attempted to fight back as best it could. Although it failed to launch any aircraft, in the first few days of fighting, several small, hand-held surface-to-air missiles were fired, and Taliban antiaircraft guns fired repeatedly.

Colonel Thomas Arko, a lieutenant colonel at the time, was commander of a B-2B bomber squadron and recalled the first night of fighting: "You could see triple-A [antiaircraft artillery] firing everywhere down below. It looked really dramatic." But it was more dramatic than dangerous: all the antiaircraft munitions were unguided. The Taliban fighters simply fired into the sky when they were under air attack.

Still, it was a dramatic night that sticks in Colonel Arko's memory. He and his unit, the 34th Bomb Squadron of the 366th Air Expeditionary Wing, had been rushed from their home base in Idaho within a week of the September 11 terrorist attacks. They soon found themselves on the island of Diego Garcia in the Indian Ocean, almost 3,000 miles (4,800 km) south of Afghanistan. Ground space on the tiny island was at such a premium that the troops were accommodated in ships docked in the harbor. The island was selected because it was home to a British military airstrip within flying range of Afghanistan, a one-way flight the big B-52 and B-2 bombers could accomplish in five or six hours. The U.S. military hastily sent as many bombers as could fit onto the island.

Lieutenant Colonel Arko and his colleagues had only enough time to establish themselves on Diego Garcia and plan their operations before they were ordered to fly the campaign's opening round of air strikes. They took off from Diego Garcia in the evening and arrived over Afghanistan some five hours later in the middle of the night. Colonel Arko recalls that the dimming of cockpit lights to combat lighting status alerted crewmembers to the fact that they had just entered Afghan airspace.

That first night, their target was a Taliban SA-13 short-range antiaircraft missile launch site at a Taliban airfield. The SA-13 was an old Soviet tactical system designed to provide point defense for army units along the front from low-flying ground-attack aircraft. In their high-tech B-2B, the 34th Expeditionary Bomb Squadron was far beyond its reach, and they released their PGMs and returned to Diego Garcia without incident.

On the second day of the air war, U.S. Defense Secretary Donald Rumsfeld explained in a television interview that the first order of business was "to remove the threat from air defenses and from Taliban aircraft. We need the freedom to operate on the ground and in the air." Rumsfeld went on to say, "... and the targets selected, if successfully destroyed, should permit an increasing degree of freedom over time." The attacks by U.S. and British forces were overwhelmingly successful. They eradicated the Taliban's small air force. "Their aircraft, to our knowledge," Rumsfeld noted, "did not leave the ground."

After the initial stage, air strikes shifted from air defenses to more widespread Taliban and al-Qaeda facilities across Afghanistan. Meanwhile, preparations for the next phase of the war were in the works: a ground campaign by the Northern Alliance.

This was the same Northern Alliance that had lost control of most of the country to the Taliban, and it had just lost its key military leader when Ahmed Massoud was assassinated. But, as Rumsfeld explained, the military campaign that was about to unfold would be unlike any war in history. Smart bombs and missiles would provide the overwhelming firepower, and elite Special Forces troops on the ground, supplied by the United States, Australia, and Britain, would provide support to the mass of Northern Alliance troops. The Pentagon was confident that this combination of firepower from above and dynamic, flexible Special Forces troops below would be enough to unhinge the Taliban. This pairing would allow the main body of Northern Alliance forces to successfully advance.

Before this daring and unique strategy could be deployed, many elements had to be prepared. More aircraft had to be moved forward to bases near Afghanistan. The war's opening air strikes had been mounted from Diego Garcia to the south and incorporated 15 B-52 bombers. U.S. Navy aircraft carriers, sailing in the northern Indian Ocean, provided additional aircraft during the opening strikes. Some of the B-2s had even flown from airbases in the continental United States, demonstrating the remarkable global reach of U.S.

KEY PLAYERS IN THE COALITION FORCE

U.S. Troops

- **Special Forces:** The exact number and composition is still classified. However, at least several hundred Special Forces ground troops were inserted into Afghanistan to work with the Northern Alliance.
- **Other Ground Forces:** In the later phases of the ground war, approximately 1,500 U.S. Marine Corps and U.S. Army Ranger troops were inserted on the ground in the Kabul and Kandahar areas.
- **Air Forces:** Various U.S. Air Force squadrons were already deployed in the Persian Gulf region, particularly in Qatar. Combat aircraft from these locations flew missions in Afghanistan, making use of air-to-air refueling. In addition, B-52 and B-2 bombers were deployed to the island of Diego Garcia in the Indian Ocean. U.S. Navy planes also flew off carriers stationed in the Indian Ocean.
- **Other Forces:** At least several dozen CIA operatives were active on the ground.

United Kingdom Troops

Some elements of 22 Squadron, the Special Air Service (SAS), were deployed with U.S. Special Forces to work with the Northern Alliance.

Australian Troops

Although these details are still classified, Australia sent several elements of its Special Forces unit, the first of which appears to have participated in the initial assault.

In addition to the above numbers, many nations have contributed forces to the subsequent international effort to stabilize Afghanistan.

Air Force air power. Nevertheless, such distances would prove prohibitive to aircraft other than the giant, intercontinental B-52s and B-2s. Additional nearby airbases were required for the longer campaign to come. Aircraft based around the Persian Gulf would be used, and—in another revolutionary development—an improvised American airbase was hastily being established in Kazakhstan, an area that was once part of the Soviet Union.

Even more important than positioning airpower was the need to place Special Forces troops on the ground. Units needed to be moved into place and set up. Working in small teams of six men, these cells would spot targets for the aircraft overhead. As critical as this was, the professional military advice and experience they would give soldiers of the Northern Alliance would be key in their attempts to coordinate the actions of the often fractious and competing local warlords of the Northern Alliance. Achieving these objectives would require several weeks.

On roughly October 19, transport air-craft began flying the necessary Special Forces ground troops into Northern Alliance territory. While this maneuver was underway, the air campaign continued: it pounded the Taliban's infrastructure and weakened its forces in prepa-ration for the unconventional ground campaign to come.

The campaign's second phase kicked into gear by redirecting its destructive force from the Taliban's rear area, where supply and support facilities were situated, to the bombing of Tal-iban troops and front-line positions. This move was the practical preparation for a ground ad-vance by the Northern Alliance. The air attacks were frequently awesome and catastrophic in their effects, and the Taliban was totally unpre-pared to face them. No force like this had been unleashed in the previous decade of grinding civil war—not even during the Soviet occupa-tion. The Soviet air bombardment, by compari-son, was scattered and inaccurate. The Afghans learned quickly that they could effectively avoid Soviet attack by moving to the hilltops and hunkering down until the aircraft passed. But they had experienced nothing like this new threat.

During the second phase of the air war, heavy bombers were used to attack ground targets in a manner that was—for them—most unorthodox. They provided close air support for the Special Forces commandos on the ground integrated with the mujahideen. The heavy bombers took flight with full loads of smart bombs but with no pre-determined targets. Upon arrival in Afghan airspace, they communicated via radio with the Special Forces patrols down on the front lines. These forces transmitted targets to the bomb crews, and bombs were released where the commandos indicated. In this way, heavy bombers could deliver precision air strikes on-call for the commandos.

In the new age of precision weapons, the Taliban's confrontation with the U.S. bombardment was something awesome and deadly.

Huge explosions ripped suddenly through the Taliban's hilltop positions. Because the bombers could release their PGMs at extremely high altitude, and because the smart bombs could glide for miles, attacks from above would often hit with no warning and when no aircraft were visible overhead. The stealthy approach of such destruction was disconcerting. When a squadron of big B-52s was sighted circling lazily and silent far overhead—completely beyond the reach of any weapon the Taliban possessed—it signaled that the inevitable hammer blows of U.S. bombs were on the way.

In late October, when Special Forces commandos arrived on the ground with the Northern Alliance militias, many began to wear tribal clothes and grow beards. Some rode out to the front lines on hardy little local horses, their radios and other target-spotting equipment carried on pack mules. These commandos quickly integrated into the Northern Alliance forces and became effective allies. In one instance, Rashid

Dostum, one of the Northern Alliance's fiercest commanders, cornered a young Special Forces lieutenant, loudly demanding more air support. A mere 20 minutes later, volleys of precision-guided bombs rained down on the positions Dostum had indicated. Explosions rocked the Taliban positions. Fireballs flashed everywhere, artillery pieces were destroyed, and some 250 Taliban fighters were cut down. Dostum was astounded. Unaccustomed to Western high-intensity warfare, he had not expected the air support to arrive for at least 24 hours.

Making war at ground level

By early November, the war had advanced to the operation's next phase: a ground advance by the Northern Alliance. The advance commenced with a move against the crucial northern city of Mazar-e-Sharif. The battle roared to life on November 9, 2001, with heavy U.S. bombing of Taliban troops concentrated in the Chesmay-e-Safa gorge just outside the entrance to the city.

Then at 2 p.m., Northern Alliance forces swept in from the south and west, seizing the city's military base and the airport. The Taliban resistance in the city collapsed, and the remaining fighters were mopped up, offering only feeble resistance. Sunset found the remaining Taliban forces retreating to the south and east. Mazar-e-Sharif was taken.

The next day, while Northern Alliance troops who had captured the city occupied themselves primarily with looting, other Northern Alliance forces swept through the northern provinces around Mazar-e-Sharif in a rapid advance. The fall of the city had triggered a complete collapse of Taliban positions. Afghanistan's regime, at the local level, was unraveling at the seams.

As often happens in war, once resistance begins to give way, the collapse quickly becomes a rout. Such was the case with the Taliban withdrawal. Disorganized groups of Taliban began to fall back through Kabul, while armed factions of the Northern Alliance, with small numbers of

U.S. and British Special Forces advisors and forward air controllers, rolled forward. Little open fighting was encountered. Wherever Northern Alliance met Taliban elements that remained in Kabul's fighting positions, devastating air strikes were called down. The Northern Alliance mujahideen then simply mopped up the shattered position. Facing this grim prospect, many local Taliban commanders took the traditional Afghan tack—they quickly switched loyalties.

By November 12, the Taliban's positions were melting away along the front lines, and late that night, the bulk of their remaining fighters slipped out of the capital under cover of darkness. When Northern Alliance forces arrived in Kabul the following afternoon, little more than bomb craters, charred foliage, and the burned-out shells of Taliban gun emplacements remained to greet them. A small group of about two dozen Arabic al-Qaeda fighters hiding in the city's park were the sole Taliban forces. After a brief 15-minute gun battle, all the foreign fighters were dead. Kabul had fallen.

The fall of the capital led, it seemed, to a general collapse of the Taliban regime. In a sudden rush by the Northern Alliance fighters, much of the rest of the country fell to their control the following day. Taliban forces, for their part, retreated to two major strongholds: Konduz in the north and Kandahar in the south. Konduz was soon besieged by the Northern Alliance, with 10,000 Taliban fighters bottled up inside.

That same day, November 13, in the mountainous Tora Bora area of eastern Afghanistan, al-Qaeda forces—and almost certainly Osama bin Laden himself—had regrouped. There, in the many caves that riddled the high mountains, the remaining Taliban fighters prepared to stand against the Northern Alliance and the U.S. forces. As many as 2,000 al-Qaeda fighters fortified themselves within the Tora Bora bunkers and caves. By November 16, U.S. bombers stepped up the bombing campaign against these targets. In an effort to cut off al-Qaeda escape routes, CIA and Special Forces personnel moved simultaneously into the area on the ground, enlisting and paying local warlords to join the fight.

Bombings at Tora Bora shifted into high gear and the bloody siege of Konduz, which began on November 16, continued. After nine days of fierce ground battles and heavy U.S. bombardment, the Taliban fighters in Konduz agreed to surrender to Northern Alliance troops.

The Taliban were herded into the Qala-e-Jangi prison complex near Mazar-e-Sharif. A handful of resistant foreign Taliban attacked the Northern Alliance guards near them, wrestled their weapons from them, and opened fire. This small success for the Taliban triggered a widespread revolt by 600 of the detained fighters at the prison. Mike Spann, a CIA agent who had been interviewing prisoners, was killed. This was the first U.S. combat death of the war.

The rebellious Taliban soon seized the southern half of the Qala-e-Jangi complex.

Control of the prison was only re-established by the Northern Alliance after three days of heavy strafing fire by U.S. AC-130 gunships and Black Hawk helicopters. Fewer than 100 of the 600 Taliban prisoners survived, and approximately 50 Northern Alliance soldiers were killed. Crushing the prison uprising marked the end of the combat in northern Afghanistan, leaving local Northern Alliance warlords firmly in control.

By the end of November, Kandahar—the Taliban's birthplace—remained the lone area in Afghanistan still under Taliban control, and it was coming under increasing pressure. Nearly 3,000 Northern Alliance and other Afghan tribal fighters backed by U.S. airpower were closing in on the city. At their head was Hamid Karzai, the westernized and polished leader of the Popalzai tribe of the Pashtuns and a former member of the Rabbani government.

At the same time, the first significant contingent of U.S. combat troops arrived. Nearly 1,000 Marines, ferried in by Chinook helicopters, set up base in the desert south of Kandahar on November 25. The first significant combat involving U.S. ground forces occurred the following day, when roughly a dozen Taliban armored vehicles advanced on the base from Kandahar; the vehicles were attacked by helicopter gunships, which destroyed most of them. Air strikes simultaneously pounded Taliban positions inside the city, where Mullah Omar was holed up. Omar remained defiant despite the fact that his movement now controlled little more than the besieged city of Kandahar itself, and he instructed his forces to fight to the death.

As the country's final Taliban stronghold teetered on the brink of defeat, U.S. forces increasingly shifted their focus to the cave complex in the Tora Bora region. On December 2, a group of U.S. commandos was inserted by helicopter to support the operation. A few days later, Afghan militia managed to advance into the area, gaining control of the foothills around the mountain caves where the al-Qaeda fighters were shut in.

The al-Qaeda fighters, mostly composed of Arabs, withdrew into the maze of caves and bunkers high in the mountains.

The final days of resistance

Meanwhile on the other side of the world a political deal was being struck for a new Afghanistan. Since November 27, at the behest of the United Nations Security Council and with the strong support of the United States, a meeting of Afghan delegates had been held at a secluded resort near the town of Bonn in western Germany. This group included Northern Alliance representatives; the former king of Afghanistan, King Muhammad Zahir Shaw; and several other parties recognized by the international community. Pointedly, no Taliban representatives were invited. On December 5, after some convoluted and hard-fought negotiations, the group produced a declaration commonly known as the Bonn Agreement. It was not a peace treaty because none of the representatives present were at war with others. But it did announce the creation of an "interim administration" for Afghanistan, and Rabbani, who was technically still the internationally recognized Afghan head of state, agreed to transfer power to this new interim authority. After some fierce backroom politicking, consensus was achieved, and it was agreed that the leader of this interim authority would be Hamid Karzai. At the time, Karzai was in Afghanistan and, along with the Northern Alliance fighters, was in the midst of the siege of the last Taliban holdouts in Kandahar. The Bonn Agreement was endorsed the following day with United Nations Security Council Resolution 1383.

On December 6, Mullah Omar signaled that he was at last prepared to surrender Kandahar to the tribal forces. His authority gone, his forces broken and scattered (hiding from the constant bombardment) his final days in Kandahar have been likened to Hitler's last days in Berlin. Reports depict him as a distraught man, at times on the verge of weeping. Recognizing that he could not hold Kandahar much longer, Mullah Omar indicated he was prepared to negotiate surrender of the city, provided that his safety and that of his top men would be guaranteed. However, the U.S. government refused to offer amnesty to Omar or any Taliban leaders. On December 7, Omar slipped from the city with a small group of hardcore loyalists and retreated northwest into the mountains of Uruzgan province. In so doing, he abandoned the remaining Taliban forces and reneged on a promise to negotiate the surrender of the fighters and their weapons. He was last seen fleeing with a group of his fighters in a convoy of motorcycles. Other members of the Taliban leadership fled into Pakistan through the remote passes of Paktia and Paktika provinces.

Two days later, on December 9, Hamid Karzai entered Kandahar in an unarmed convoy. The city was sullen and silent, and the Taliban had melted away. Pockets of hard-core al-Qaeda remained holed up and steadfast in the mountain caves of Tora Bora, where operations against them continued. Nevertheless, the Taliban regime had effectively been toppled from power in Afghanistan. On December 16, U.S. Secretary of State Colin Powell declared, "We have ended the role of Afghanistan as a haven for terrorist activity."

The nature of the war

Unlike most U.S. military operations, the one that knocked the Taliban regime from power in Afghanistan was launched from a virtual standstill, a cold start. At all times, the U.S. military maintains many "contingency plans"—theoretical plans for how it would fight a war, should one break out. These are often called "war plans" in the popular press, but the official military term is *conplan,* an abbreviation of contingency plan. Scenarios that present serious risks and represent probable conflicts—North Korea, for example—have more than one conplan established, so that the United States can respond quickly and flexibly as different scenarios unfold.

Quite remarkably, no blueprint existed for the unfolding Operation Enduring Freedom. No conplan had been predetermined. Prior to September 11, 2001, Afghanistan was, for the most part, a forgotten and neglected backwater. Beyond plans for the possible deployment of long-range cruise missile strikes of the sort used to discipline al-Qaeda before, Afghanistan appears to have attracted sparse attention from U.S. military planners. Even more tellingly is the fact that the United States had no pre-positioned forces near Afghanistan and no easy way to reach this mountainous and land-locked country in central Asia.

Yet within 26 days of the al-Qaeda attacks on the World Trade Center towers and Washington, D.C., the U.S. military launched an operation from half a world away that—in just over two months—succeeded in routing resistance and establishing an interim government. The Soviet Union, from relative proximity, had failed to achieve this goal, as had the British and countless empires before that. Even the Afghan mujahideen, themselves, had found this an impossible task.

CHAPTER 5

Mopping Up:
The Tora Bora Stronghold

Victory and a new government had been declared halfway around the world at the Bonn Conference, but in the mountains of Afghanistan the fighting continued. With the departure of Mullah Omar, the Taliban was a spent force. Nevertheless, thousands of al-Qaeda fighters remained in the country. Most critically, Osama bin Laden was still at large with the remnants of his forces.

After the fall of Kandahar, bin Laden and the majority of al-Qaeda troops retreated into the mountains of eastern Afghanistan. There, bordering the tribal regions of Pakistan, al-Qaeda established a complex of caves and bunkers, as well as stashes of weapons, ammunition, and supplies. The legend of these bunkers has embellished, producing outlandish claims of vast underground complexes complete with hotel-like accommodation for thousands of troops, air ventilation systems, and even generators that produce electrical power by harnessing underground streams.

In fact, secretive and opulent James Bond-like lairs did not exist. The bunkers and caves, however, were quite real. They were a collection of crude, roughly hewn hiding places and caches that provided sufficient room to accommodate the approximately 1,500 to 2,000 al-Qaeda fighters who had retreated there. Bin Laden had fought the Soviets from Tora Bora; with secret Pakistani support, his followers had fought the original Rabbani government from there, as well. Now, as his Taliban allies collapsed, bin Laden returned.

This was not surprising. U.S. intelligence had long ago identified this al-Qaeda base camp, and the new Karzai government was painfully aware of its strength there. Even as the new Afghan Interim Government established itself and put down roots in Kabul, military planning turned toward the al-Qaeda mountain redoubt.

The first strike, as always in this new model of warfare, came from the air. U.S. bombers began to pound the cave entrances, even while more detailed planning was underway and ground forces marshaled for a push into the daunting landscape. But caves and deep bunkers are difficult targets to bomb effectively. For this, the latest specialized "bunker-buster" bombs were deployed. In addition, heavy conventional bombs, such as the BLU-82, nicknamed the "Daisy Cutter," were employed. These powerful bombs, when paired with the newest precision guidance technology, could be dropped onto the cave and bunker access points. On occasion, they could be angled to plunge down the entrance shafts before detonating. The explosions inside the confines of the interiors would cause grievous damage to the human inhabitants as well as collapse the entrance beneath tons of rock.

An additional tactic U.S. air power developed for this phase of the war was the pairing of bombers with AC-130 gunships. The bombers orbited high overhead and guided bombs down onto all the known or suspected entrances along one side of a mountain or ridge. Meanwhile, the AC-130 gunships circled in wait over the far side of the ridge. As al-Qaeda fighters streamed from the bunker and cave entrances, fleeing the devastating bombing, the Specter gunships would open up with rockets and machine guns.

By December 8, ground forces had pushed their way up from Kabul to join the fight. A collection of Northern Alliance ground troops traded shots with the al-Qaeda rear guard as they sought to protect the few rough tracks that led into the mountains. U.S. Special Forces patrols pushed forward with their Afghan allies and guided many of the air strikes. By December 10, the al-Qaeda fighters, realizing the futility of their position and claiming to be reluctant to fight fellow Muslims, called for a cease-fire to arrange their surrender.

In retrospect, this truce was likely a ruse to enable the bulk of the al-Qaeda remnants to escape. It should be remembered that most of the fighting in the war had not taken the form of pitched battles in which a decisive victory or defeat was determined by force. Rather, most fighting consisted of exchanges of gunfire until it became clear which side held the upper hand; at that point, the combatants that recognized their losing position would either withdraw or simply switch sides. Truces were therefore a common practice, and the local mujahideen commanders duly accepted the proposal by the al-Qaeda forces as standard practice. However, the battles that served as models for the surrender of one side to another had been fought by rival Afghan factions. This, conversely, was a battle with al-Qaeda soldiers. Most of these fighters were Arabic and not Afghan and all of them were fanatical in their purpose, not pragmatic tribal warriors of past conflicts. In the end, no al-Qaeda forces came down out of the mountains to surrender, and on December 12, fighting flared again as Northern Alliance forces lost patience and pushed farther into the Tora Bora range.

On December 17, the last cave complex was captured, but only 200 al-Qaeda fighters were accounted for, almost all of whom were dead. The bulk of the foreign jihadists had somehow snuck away. Most importantly, Osama bin Laden remained at large.

At a Pentagon news conference that December, Rear Admiral John Stufflebeem spoke about the hunt for bin Laden, saying: "I'm not

sure how close we ever really have been. We
have narrowed it down to an area. Indicators
were there, and now indicators are not there. So
maybe he still is here, maybe he was killed, or
maybe he's left."

In hindsight, it now appears bin Laden spir-
ited himself across the border into Pakistan, accompanied by at least 1,000 al-Qaeda fighters.

The tribal areas of Pakistan

Afghanistan's northeastern border with Pakistan
is a particularly troublesome area. As a mountainous, thinly populated, and remote location,
it is difficult to control—making it an excellent
setting in which guerrillas and other fugitives
can hide. This site is also noteworthy because of
the socio-political nature of the region that lies
just across the border in Pakistan. The region's
tribal populace has a long history of self-deter-
mined independence.

The modern state of Pakistan was formed
in 1947 and was carved out of what was the

British colony of India. When the British withdrew from India and granted it independence, they attempted to negotiate a transition that would sustain the region as a whole and enable it to become a democratic, stable, and prosperous nation. However, while much of the Indian independence movement had been led by a pacifist—Mahatma Gandhi—very considerable currents of ethnic and religious strife saturated the colony as it moved into nationhood. The most critical of these disputes lay between religious Hindus and religious Muslims. Although both religious factions lived throughout much of the country, Hindus far outnumbered Muslims. Moreover, Muslims sought an independent country of their own. Naturally, the Muslim independence movement found its greatest strength and deepest roots in geographic areas where Muslims represented the cultural majority, and the largest such region lay in the northwest. The British determined that the expanse would become the nation of Pakistan. This was also the old "North-West Frontier," over which the British had fought three Anglo-Afghan wars and through which the Durand line ran.

Just as the North-West Frontier had been difficult for the British Raj to control, so, too, was it difficult for the new Pakistani government to rule. When Pakistan was established, it was divided into four provinces with a federal government located in the capital, Islamabad. However, the North-West Frontier proved so unruly that it was not designated a province; instead, it was established as a territory that would be administered directly by the federal government. In practice, however, it was scarcely ruled at all. The territory was identified officially as the Federally Administered Tribal Areas, a moniker that reflected the reality that traditional, local tribes effectively governed the region with little interference from official Pakistani authorities. Just as they did with the British Raj a century ago, contemporary tribes in the territory guarded their independence jealously from what they perceived as outside rule.

The consequence is that the area—in legal and military terms—is at best poorly controlled, at least from the perspective of outside governments and agencies. As a Muslim area and home to many suspicious of the non-Muslim West, it was an especially suitable hideaway for al-Qaeda.

The International Security Assistance Force

Just as operations under U.S. leadership were winding up in the Tora Bora area, the international community came to Afghanistan in the form of the International Security Assistance Force (ISAF). This international force was authorized by the United Nations Security Council, but it was not run as a UN operation. The first six-month ISAF mission was undertaken by the British, the second by the Turks, and the third by the Germans and Dutch. In the summer of 2003, NATO took leadership of the ISAF mission, which aimed to provide security and a stabilizing force in the country, even as U.S.-led operations to root out terrorists continued. The aim remains that ISAF will lead the "defensive" effort to stabilize the country as the U.S. leads the "offensive" effort to track down and stamp out the remaining Taliban and al-Qaeda constituents and other terrorist elements. This simultaneous two-track approach continues today.

In practice, ISAF's initial operations were confined to the capital city of Kabul, which prompted some criticism that its objectives were not sufficiently comprehensive. ISAF fielded a multinational brigade of more than 4,000 soldiers in Kabul, and it assumed control of Kabul International Airport. The first commander of ISAF was British Major General John McColl. Significant troop contributions came from Britain, as well as Canada, Italy, Germany, and France. At the same time, the U.S. Operation Enduring Freedom continued in other parts of the country, notably in the east and south along the border with Pakistan. In some cases, nations contributed troops to ISAF, under international command and directed by a UN mandate, while simultaneously providing additional troops—specifically Special Forces with greater offensive capabilities—to the U.S.-led Operation Enduring Freedom.

Commando operations

An excellent example of the sort of commando operations mounted by these Special Forces occurred in February 2002. The operation kicked off with a single terse report dispatched via satellite phone: "Mullah K has left the building."

"Mullah K" was Mullah Khairullah Kahirkhawa, an elusive, high-ranked Taliban official the United States had actively searched for since the Mullah Omar's surrender two months earlier. Now he had been spotted by one of the unmanned spy-plane drones that flew over the country. The surveillance drone, known as a "Predator," is remotely operated by radio control, similar to that of a model aircraft, except that the Predator has a wingspan of 50 feet (15 m), a range of 400 miles (640 km), and can remain in the air for more than six hours. It carries various surveillance devices and cameras, and it radios images back to its operators at a ground control station.

The exact location of the ground control station was classified, but it was likely Bagram airbase. That day, on the flickering TV screens in the control room the drone's cameras revealed Mullah Kahirkhawa leaving a mud-brick house high in the hills of eastern Afghanistan. He climbed into the cab of a truck, one of several in a convoy of battered pick-up trucks. This was what they had been watching for, and the operators quickly phoned the commandos: "Mullah K has left the building. He's on the move."

The call went to U.S. Navy Captain Robert Harward, the commanding officer of the Special Forces unit that had been established for southern Afghanistan. Harward was one of the famous Navy SEALs—the Navy's branch of

Special Forces commandos—and the unit he commanded was officially known as the Combined Joint Special Task Force South. But everyone called this team "Task Force K-Bar," named after a type of commando knife. Harward's headquarters was located at the new U.S. base, Camp Rhino, just outside Kandahar. Camp Rhino comprised nearly 3,000 Special Forces personnel that included special operations forces from Canada, Norway, Denmark, Germany, Australia, New Zealand, and Turkey, in addition to the Americans.

"We planned, designed, and executed that operation with one hour's notice," Harward said in an interview later in 2002. "Once we heard he was moving, my guys went off and put together a plan in 30 minutes. And 30 minutes later, it was all over. The whole operation—coordinating 40 U.S. and Danish Special Forces—was a great example of how all the training we've had in combined and joint operations can work and succeed in the field." The effort involved U.S.

Air Force Special Forces, Danish Special Forces, U.S. Navy SEALs, and U.S. Army helicopters. "It was a real testament to teaming," said Harward, of the elimination of Mullah K.

The mission to capture Mullah Khairullah Kahirkhawa was one of more than 75 missions performed by Task Force K-Bar between October 2001 and April 2002, during which time Harward served as its commanding officer. The operations Harward oversaw were among the most sensitive and dangerous in Afghanistan. One mission, conducted in early January, was to investigate the al-Qaeda hideout at Zhawar Kili. It was expected to last 12 hours, but the mission turned into an eight-day ordeal, as U.S. forces scoured the 70-cave complex adjacent to Pakistan. Another mission involved a days-long surveillance and subsequent raid of Ali Kheyl, a multi-storied medieval fortress perched at 14,000 feet near the city of Khost in eastern Afghanistan. As a result of the success of these missions, Task Force K-Bar was award-ed a Presidential Unit Citation. The award was presented to the Task Force on the same day that Hamid Karzai was sworn in as president of Afghanistan.

The Taliban and al-Qaeda adapt

Following the defeat of the al-Qaeda band at Tora Bora, U.S. forces and their Afghan allies consolidated their military and political authority in the country. Following a *loya jirga*—a grand council—of major Afghan factions, tribal leaders, and former exiles, an interim Afghan government was established in Kabul under Hamid Karzai. U.S. forces dug in for the long haul at Bagram air base, their main staging area just north of Kabul. Kandahar airport also became an important U.S. base. Several outposts were established in eastern provinces to hunt for Taliban and al-Qaeda fugitives, and the number of U.S.-led coalition troops operating in the country would eventually grow beyond 10,000.

The Taliban and al-Qaeda, however, had not yet given up. Throughout January and February 2002, al-Qaeda forces regrouped in the Shahi-Kot Mountains of Paktia province. Mullah Saifur Rehman, a Taliban fugitive in the area, also began reconstituting his militia forces to support the foreign fighters. All told, they totaled more than 1,000 men by early March. The rebels' intended to use the region as a base for launching guerrilla attacks and, with careful planning, a major offensive in the style of the mujahideen who battled the Soviets during the 1980s.

U.S. and allied Afghan militia intelligence sources soon caught wind of this activity in Paktia province. During a massive push on March 2, 2002, U.S. and Afghan forces launched an offensive against al-Qaeda and Taliban fighters entrenched in the mountains of Shahi-Kot, southeast of Gardez. The rebel forces, which used small arms, rocket-propelled grenades, and mortars, were entrenched in caves and bunkers in the hillsides. They employed "hit-and-run" tactics—opening fire on the U.S. and Afghan forces and then retreating into their caves and bunkers to weather the return fire and persistent U.S. bombing raids. The circumstances were made worse for the coalition troops because U.S. commanders initially underestimated the number of Taliban and al-Qaeda forces present, assessing the opposition as a final, isolated pocket of 200 or so dead-enders. In reality, the guerrillas numbered at least 1,000 and perhaps as many as 5,000, according to some estimates—and they were gaining reinforcements.

By March 6, eight Americans and seven Afghan soldiers had been killed, while a reported 400 opposition forces had been neutralized in the exchange. The coalition casualties stemmed from the downing of two helicopters by rocket-propelled grenades and small arms fire that killed seven soldiers and a friendly fire incident that killed one soldier. In addition, U.S. forces were pinned down while being inserted into a target, coined "Objective Ginger," and the result was dozens of wounded. Ultimately, ground fire from Afghan militia and American forces in a number of skirmishes, combined with heavy aerial bombardment, generated over 400 al-Qaeda and Taliban rebel deaths, according to U.S. estimates. However, fewer than 50 bodies were found. Regardless of the correct number of enemy casualties, it was clear several hundred combatants had escaped the dragnet by moving in small groups along mountain trails to tribal areas across the Pakistani border. Pakistani armed forces that were supposed to confront and block these forces apparently lacked either the will or the capability—possibly both—to seal the border.

Following the battle at Shahi-Kot, it is believed that al-Qaeda fighters established sanctuaries among tribal protectors in Pakistan. Here they regained their strength and began to launch cross-border raids on U.S. forces in the summer months of 2002. Even today, guerrilla units numbering between 5 and 25 men continue to regularly cross the border to fire rockets at U.S. bases and to ambush U.S. convoys and patrols, Afghan National Army troops, Afghan militia forces working with the U.S-led coalition, and non-governmental organizations. The area around the U.S. base at Shkin, in Paktika province, has been the site of some of the heaviest insurgent activity of the war.

Taliban forces also remained in hiding in the rural regions of the four southern provinces that formed their heartland: Kandahar, Zabul, Helmand, and Uruzgan. In the wake of Operation Anaconda, which entailed mopping up in the Tora Bora area, the Pentagon requested the deployment of British Royal Marines, who are highly trained in mountain warfare. The Royal Marines conducted a number of missions over several weeks, but these produced limited results. The Taliban, who numbered in the hundreds in the summer of 2002, sought to avoid outright combat with the United States and its Afghan allies: Taliban fighters retreated into remote mountain-range caves and tunnels or slipped into Pakistan during these operations. The consequence was a number of fruitless missions conducted by U.S. and British forces, during which no combat occurred and no enemy forces were captured or killed. Even with the support of local inhabitants—and it's not clear to what extent the coalition actually had this support—and despite advanced surveillance technology that could locate small bands of 5 to 10 men in the vast stretches of rugged terrain of Afghanistan's southeastern border, Taliban and al-Qaeda forces managed to avoid contact. These circumstances persisted for the remainder of 2002.

By evading U.S. forces throughout that summer, the Taliban remnants gradually rebuilt their numbers and regained confidence. They began preparations for the insurgency Mullah Muhammad Omar had pledged to deliver during the Taliban's last days in power. In September, Taliban forces initiated a recruitment drive in Pashtun areas of Afghanistan and Pakistan. They sought to launch a renewed holy war (jihad) against the Afghan government and the U.S.-led coalition. Pamphlets calling for jihad were distributed in secret during the night, appearing in villages throughout the former Taliban heartland of southeastern Afghanistan. According to Afghan sources and a United Nations report, it was at this time that al-Qaeda and Taliban fugitives constructed small, mobile training camps along the Pakistan border, in order to train new recruits in guerrilla warfare and terrorist tactics. The majority of new recruits were drawn from the *madrassas*, or religious schools, set up in Pakistani tribal areas from which the Taliban, themselves, had first arisen.

By the summer of 2003, major bases, a few with as many as 200 men, were erected in the mountainous tribal areas. Slipping across the long, ragged border in small groups proved a relatively simple task, despite consistent patrolling by security forces. Again, the will of Pakistani paramilitary forces stationed at border crossings to prevent such travel was dubious at best, and Pakistani military operations guaranteed neither safety nor opposition.

The Taliban slowly but productively restructured and repopulated its forces over the winter months, as it prepared for a summer offensive. It also developed a new modus operandi: in groups of roughly 50, it launched attacks on isolated outposts and on convoys of Afghan soldiers, police, or militia. It would then devolve into groups of 5 to 10 men, in order to evade counterattacks.

This strategy, however, inevitably brought Taliban fighters into more consistent combat with international forces—and their superior firepower. The consequence was heavy Taliban casualties, particularly during engagements that involved as many as 100 rebel fighters.

It is unknown how many Taliban were killed in such skirmishes. The U.S. military has refused to be drawn into "body count" speculations, as occurred in Vietnam, but the numbers probably exceed 1,000—enough to significantly reduce the number of hard-core fighters the Taliban could hope to field.

What is absolutely clear is that as a result of growing casualty rates, the Taliban shifted its insurgency strategy in 2004. Previously, Taliban rebels had fought in a fundamentally conventional style—albeit in a light infantry or guerrilla fashion: essentially, they maintained open positions, even if those positions were hidden in the mountains. The Taliban maneuvered around the battlefield in an effort to capture a given town or a strategic village and to defeat the force that opposed it. This line of attack now changed. Unable to absorb the mounting casualties, the Taliban shifted the nature and emphasis of its operations to terrorist-type tactics and practices.

The Taliban now focused not on battles but on hit-and-run attacks. Its violence predominantly targeted soft-targets: civilians, Afghan

government officials, and the cohorts of international agencies.

CHAPTER 6

Rebuilding Afghanistan

Hamid Karzai had been named the head of the new Afghan regime by the Bonn Conference in December 2001, but at the time he was given the carefully crafted title of Interim Administration Head. Pointedly, neither the term "government" nor a designation such as president, prime minister, or a traditional Afghan label was granted. There was a strong desire all around to stress that the Bonn

declaration was only an interim measure that
would last until a democratically elected government could be formed. Combined with the
principle involved in this decision, there was
the pragmatic matter of ensuring the new government was widely recognized and accepted.
The Taliban had been recognized by only Pakistan, Saudi Arabia, and a handful of other Muslim states. There was also a concern among
Afghans that they not be perceived as merely
the puppets of the United States.

The first step in this process was to create a
properly established transitional government. It
would take time to organize a working constitution and hold full, democratic elections across
the country in parts where military operations
were ongoing. To set up a transitional government, a special grand assembly with representatives from across the country was held. The
loya jirga was conducted in a giant tent on the
grounds of Kabul Polytechnic University, beginning June 11, 2002. The assembly deliberated

for more than a week and eventually achieved consensus on the general structure and naming of what was officially entitled the Afghan Transitional Administration.

As expected, Hamid Karzai was named president of the transitional administration, and many key appointments went to senior Northern Alliance members. The important portfolio of defense minister went to Fahim Khan, who had succeeded Ahmed Shah Massoud as the senior Northern Alliance military commander when the latter was assassinated September 9, 2001. Perhaps the greatest surprise was that Ismail Khan was not named to an appointment in the central government (although his son became minister of air transportation). Instead, Ismail Khan became governor of Herat province, his old power base. Some feared that this major regional warlord remaining governor of his established power base rather than joining the new government was an ominous sign. They were concerned that events might repeat the pattern of the mujahideen government of 1992 through 1996, when squabbling between regional warlords led to civil war and the rise of the Taliban.

Overall, however, the 2002 loya jirga was a great success. Held a mere six months after the fall of the Taliban regime, it established a framework that effectively prevented civil war, and it laid the foundation for a transitional government that was able to move toward rebuilding the political and administrative systems of Afghanistan.

LOYA JIRGA

A term from the Pashtun language, loya means "great" or "grand," and jirga means "council," "assembly," or "meeting." Loya jirgas are a traditional Afghan mechanism that historians can trace back many centuries. Certainly, loya jirgas have been employed by Afghan rulers as far back as the 18th century. Loya jirgas tend to include tribal, military, and religious figures, in addition to royalty and central government officials. Traditionally, decisions are made by consensus, and no formal votes are taken. There are no time limits within which a loya jirga must be conducted, and it continues until decisions are reached.

The support of outside nations

One reason for the success of the loya jirga was the arrival in Kabul of the International Security Assistance Force, or ISAF. ISAF's international peacekeeping mission was authorized by United Nations Security Council Resolution 1386 on December 20, 2001. The mission, which was established for a six-month period, was "To assist the Afghan Interim Authority in the maintenance of security in Kabul and its surrounding areas, so that the Afghan Interim Authority as well as the personnel of the United Nations [could] operate in a secure environment."

While the UN created ISAF, the mission itself was not run as a UN operation. Instead, the Security Council "invited" the member states of the UN to volunteer to form ISAF and authorized them "to take all necessary measures to fulfill" ISAF's mandate—the classic diplomatic wording that allows for the use of war or deadly force. The first such "volunteer" was Great Britain. It sent Major General John McColl as the first commander, and the military forces that made up the core of the first mission, along with contributions from many other nations. The six-month term was subsequently transformed into a rolling six-month rotation of units.

Although essentially confined to the Kabul area and initially widely criticized as a force that lacked a clear mandate beyond meddling in the affairs of Afghanistan, ISAF did succeed in keeping the peace. Given the fractious history of Afghanistan, simply preventing the outright resumption of civil war was a great achievement. In any event, ISAF gave the transitional government the crucial breathing room necessary to establish itself.

On the road to government

The second step down the path to a stable and legitimate government was the writing and ratification of a new constitution for the country. Once again, this was to be done by a loya jirga. Regional representatives were elected in local elections across the country. Tribal groups and other organizations also appointed delegates. Sixty-four female delegates were chosen specifically to represent women's interests; as well, 42 delegates were named to represent refugees and other displaced persons. Karzai directly appointed 50 delegates. In all, 502 delegates convened in Kabul on December 14, 2003. After some bruising debate in which disputes centered primarily on the relative positions of the represented ethnic groups, the assembly ratified a new constitution on January 4, 2004. The new constitution provided for a directly elected president as head of state, a position fortified with strong central powers. The president is both the head of state and the head of government. There is also a legislature with two parts: a *Wolesi Jirga,* or House of People (similar to the U.S. Congress), whose members are directly elected for a five-year term, and the *Meshrano Jirga,* or House of Elders (which is similar to the U.S. Senate).

Elections for the presidency were scheduled for July 5, 2004, only six months after the ratification of the new constitution. Twenty-three candidates registered for the election, although five of them withdrew during the campaign. The clear front-runner from the outset was interim leader Hamid Karzai, who registered himself as an independent candidate not associated with a specific party. Pursuing the theme he had championed since his selection as interim leader at the Bonn Conference, he identified himself as a unifying figure that could reach out to all of Afghanistan's tribal groups.

Rashid Dostum, the northern warlord who had switched allegiances so many times in the past, was one of Karzai's high-profile challengers. Despite his leading role in the Northern Alliance as a successful military commander in the campaign to oust the Taliban, Dostum's complicated political history—not to mention his reputation for brutality on the battlefield—worked against him. He did not attract widespread support beyond that which originated in his traditional power base around Mazar-e-Sharif.

Two other significant candidates ran: Yunus Qanuni and Mohammed Mohaqiq, both veteran Afghan politicians who had been prominent in the Northern Alliance and the old Rabbani government. Qanuni claimed to represent the legacy of the assassinated leader Ahmed Shah Massoud, although other candidates made similar claims. Significantly, Qanuni had the support of Massoud's deputy, Muhammad Qasim Fahim, who led the military command of the Northern Alliance after the Lion of the Panjshir's death. Mohammed Mohaqiq, for his part, was a leader of the Wahdat faction of the Afghan Islamic Unity Party; he had been a government minister under Burhanuddin Rabbani and he was a strong ally of Rashid Dostum.

The elections were twice postponed—first to September and then to October 9. The Taliban and other insurgents vowed to disrupt the elections, and many pessimists predicted the election process would fail. Ultimately, widespread security precautions proved effective, and greater than 75 percent of Afghans turned out to vote—a rate that puts many Western democracies to shame. Inevitably, there were irregularities and some criticism of the voting processes and legitimacy, but the election was surprisingly successful overall. The election ran under international supervision through an organization known as the Joint Electoral Management Body. After accusations of fraud and other irregularities were made early in the campaign, the United Nations appointed a three-person oversight panel to monitor the election and rule on its fairness and legitimacy. The panel comprised a retired Canadian diplomat, a Swedish electoral expert, and a European Union official. Their official findings were that the irregularities that did occur were minor and that the result represented, unquestionably, the democratic wishes of the Afghan people.

Hamid Karzai won 55 percent of the vote

The September 2005 Election

CANDIDATE* (ETHNIC GROUP)	PARTY OR POLITICAL GROUP	NUMBER OF VOTES	PERCENTAGE OF VOTES CAPTURED
Hamid Karzai (Pashtun)	Independent	4,443,029	55.4 percent
Yunus Qanuni (Tajik)	Afghan Nationalist Party	1,306,503	16.3 percent
Mohammed Mohaqiq (Hazara)	Independent (Wahdat Islamic Unity Party)	935,325	11.7 percent
Abdul Rashid Dostum (Uzbek)	Independent (National Islamic Movement)	804,861	10.0 percent

* Fourteen other candidates ran, none of whom won more than 1.5 percent of the vote.

on the first ballot—a percentage more than three times greater than his closest competitor. Karzai was thus confirmed as the democratic leader of a new Afghanistan, and he became the country's first directly elected president.

The third and final step in the process of establishing the new, democratically elected

government for Afghanistan was to hold elections for the legislative assembly, the Wolesi
Jirga. These were held on September 18, 2005.
They, too, were successful, but only approximately 50 percent of voters turned out—a result
that likely reflected the diminished drama of an
election in which the leadership of the country
was not at stake. Afghanistan now had a func-
tioning, democratically elected government.
This was no small achievement in a country
with such a strife-ridden past.

The hunt for Osama bin Laden

The great disappointment of Operation Enduring Freedom was the failure to capture Osama
bin Laden. The U.S. government has down-
played the significance of his escape in light of
bin Laden's connection with al-Qaeda and the
September 2001 attacks in the United States,
but bin Laden's capture was indubitably a principal objective of the entire venture.

The last confirmed sighting of bin Laden

occurred near Jalabad just before the collapse of the Taliban regime. Al-Qaeda had maintained several of its camps in the Jalabad area, and it allowed a Western journalist to visit one of its secret underground facilities there. The reporter was blindfolded and brought to a bunker, where he briefly met bin Laden so that the al-Qaeda leader could issue a denunciation of the U.S.-led offensive. The reporter did not see bin Laden again, and a few days later the area fell to the advancing Northern Alliance.

It is generally believed that bin Laden retreated with his al-Qaeda forces, retiring either toward Kandahar or to the mountain hideouts of the Tora Bora region. Although al-Qaeda had maintained several camps around Kandahar, including a particularly large one at Tarnak Farm where Taliban leader Mullah Omar also had a private retreat, no sign of bin Laden was found in the area.

With the benefit of hindsight, most analysts now believe bin Laden escaped to the Tora Bora mountains and from there slipped across the border into the poorly controlled, remote, and mountainous tribal area of Pakistan.

Shortly after the consolidation of the Tora Bora area, Western intelligence agencies were concerned that bin Laden might slip even farther away, perhaps to Africa. He still had many supporters in the Sudan, where he had spent many years. It was thought that Somalia, too, was a possible destination. Somalia had a large Muslim population and was, as Afghanistan had been under the Taliban, a failing state with weak governmental control and limited contact with the outside world. Perhaps it was the sort of place to which bin Laden would withdraw. Yemen, as well, was another prospect.

There was also concern about the number of ways bin Laden could reach those destinations from Afghanistan's tribal areas. A traditional smugglers' route led from the region down to coastal Pakistan. From there, countless small boats and traditional Arabic *dhows* carried small amounts of cargo across the slender Straits of Hormuz. Much of that cargo is contraband; little, if any, is ever seen by authorities. Of greater concern, is the fact that much of the contraband cargo is human—poor, young men from Pakistan and Afghanistan looking for work in oil-rich Gulf sheikdoms, such as the United Arab Emirates (U.A.E.). They hoped to find jobs doing menial labor and then send their wages home. How difficult would it be, Western officials wondered, for bin Laden, dressed in non-descript clothes, to join that anonymous current of humanity and cross the Straits of Hormuz? Once in Oman or the U.A.E., he could easily move farther south and west into Yemen—where the bin Laden family still had connections—or across the narrow Red Sea to the Horn of Africa.

The Pentagon was sufficiently concerned about this possibility to establish a considerable naval force in the Gulf of Oman. Many coalition countries contributed ships to this force—among them most of the European NATO nations, Japan, and Canada. They occupied themselves by attempting to monitor the countless small boats darting across the Straits—a daunting task at the best of times. No sign of any al-Qaeda members was detected, much less bin Laden himself.

More significant than the international force's failure to find bin Laden is that no indications of bin Laden's presence in Yemen, the Sudan, or Somalia have ever come to light. It is generally thought that if he had made his way to one of those places, at least some whisper of his presence would find its way to the hungry eyes and ears of a Western intelligence organization. By all accounts, no such whisper has disturbed this prolonged silence.

A March 2003 incident highlights the U.S. frustration with their hunt for bin Laden. According to various reports, the CIA thought at the time that it had come close to capturing bin Laden. CIA operatives in Rawalpindi, Pakistan, working with local authorities had stormed a private villa and captured Khalid Shaikh Mohammed, a man believed to rank third within the al-Qaeda hierarchy. Pakistani authorities captured Mohammed's laptop computer and satellite phone. At last, the CIA hoped, the stalled hunt for the al-Qaeda ringleaders had gained momentum. This breakthrough could help them track down bin Laden. Analysts in Washington speculated that news of Mohammed's capture might even prompt bin Laden to flee his current hideout and thus make him more vulnerable to detection and capture.

According to one FBI official, Mohammed, in the weeks before his arrest, had been moving from one place to another in Baluchistan, a lawless province in western Pakistan. Bin Laden, it was thought, might be in the same area.

A few days later, U.S. intelligence satellites traced a telephone call made from Iran to Baluchistan by Saad bin Laden, one of Osama bin Laden's sons. While bin Laden himself no longer used phones, perhaps one of his aides had.

An unmanned surveillance drone dispatched to the region spotted a suspicious convoy moving at night. It consisted of about 100 people on horseback and on foot, and it was advancing along an ancient smugglers' route, one of many that ran through the area. U.S. officials hoped that bin Laden might be traveling with this group.

A team composed of CIA operatives, Army Special Forces commandos, and Pakistani intelligence officials descended on the convoy.

"The CIA was very confident: they thought they had him there in Baluchistan, across from the Afghan border," Vincent Cannistraro, a former chief of operations for the CIA's Counter-Terrorism Center, observed. "They had a fixed location on him. They mounted a moderate-sized operation."

The convoy was duly intercepted on the ground. Each traveler was examined. "Lo and behold, bin Laden wasn't there," Cannistraro reported. The convoy was just another group of refugees.

Iranian officials have issued a statement denying that bin Laden's son was ever in the country. U.S. officials have declined to officially acknowledge the incident at all. The search for this elusive terrorist continues.

Geologists who have examined the rock formations that are seen in the background of the most recent bin Laden videos dating from 2004, have suggested the stone is characteristic of the Khost area of Afghanistan. This region lies near Tora Bora on the mountainous border with Pakistan in one of the most politically unstable parts of the country. However, most analysts seem to agree bin Laden is now probably somewhere in the wild tribal areas of Pakistan.

Wherever he is, he remains the most hunted man on earth, with millions of dollars of bounty on his head. If he's not dead yet, he won't be able to remain in hiding forever.

Counter-insurgency:
Forward Operating Base Lagman

One of the U.S. units engaged in the "offensive" portion of the effort in Afghanistan is 2nd Battalion (Airborne) of the 503rd Infantry Regiment. In late 2005, this unit worked from Forward Operating Base (FOB) Lagman in the southern province of Zabol.

FOB Lagman sits on a towering hill overlooking an immense mud wall that had once served as a stronghold for the army of Alexander the Great. Today, the site is the home of a U.S. battalion group under the command of Lieutenant Colonel Mark Stammer. Known as Task Force Rock (TF Rock), the airborne battalion had been reorganized in connection with specific attachments and sent to Afghanistan to assist the new Afghan government in its efforts to root out Taliban resistance. The battalion is spread out over nine bases, with the main camp and battalion headquartered at FOB Lagman in the city of Qalat. The site at Lagman was the first permanent U.S. presence in the province and served as a visible, tangible sign of American strength in the area.

For Lieutenant Colonel Mark Stammer, the mission was clear. His unit would be responsible for establishing order and returning the rule of law to the government. It was a considerable task given the tremendous tension in the area, but Stammer was optimistic that his troops were up to the assignment. The coalition presence in the region was robust, and he had the trust and respect of the local tribal leaders.

TF Rock is made up of three infantry companies and a headquarters company, as well as the battalion headquarters. The headquarters company, affectionately known as the Black Sheep, comprises the support trades—the cooks, medics, and truck drivers who keep the task force going. The real work of the unit, though, is done by the dusty foot soldiers of the three infantry companies. Each company, with about 100 soldiers, patrols a specific area.

Able Company, or "the Warlords," are responsible for daily operations in the plains of the province's southern districts. This proved to be a particularly perilous region because insurgents commonly employed the use of roadside bombs. The northern districts of the province are, for the most part, impassable by vehicle, so the men of Battle Company, or "Battle Hard," perform the most physically demanding patrolling, traversing the hills and mountains with 90-pound (50-kg) rucksacks on their backs. Chosen Company, or "the Punishers," conducts patrols in convoys of armored Humvees alongside squads of Afghan soldiers or police in the more populated middle area.

Danger faces the men of Task Force Rock on a daily basis. While the enemy often decides it's not beneficial to engage the Americans in open combat, they can be deadly foes when on the offensive. Over the course of seven months in 2005, Lieutenant Colonel Stammer and his battalion faced insurgents in over 200 skirmishes:

25 incidents involved roadside bombings, 40 were rocket or mortar attacks, and more than 135 incidents involved direct fire. While most of these were brief efforts to ambush patrols, TF Rock fought several more sustained actions with insurgent forces. May 3, 2005, was one such encounter.

Battle at the village of Kharnay

For nearly a month, seven-man scouting teams from the battalion had been gathering intelligence in the small village of Gazak in the Khaki Afghan District. They heard from the locals that large Taliban forces were assembling in the village of Kharnay, which lay 10 miles (16 km) farther to the south. The decision was made to make the two-hour journey to investigate this intelligence. With a medic and an interpreter, 14 members of the Afghan National Police accompanied the seven-man team. The route was treacherous, cutting through nearly impassable terrain. The real danger, however, became apparent when they arrived in Kharnay. There, they found an old Afghan man bleeding on the side of the road.

The translator quickly asked the beaten man what had happened. He exclaimed frantically and waved to the road in front of them.

"They are just down this road, in the very next village," he yelled anxiously, almost breathless.

Squad leader Staff Sergeant Brannan peered down the road, his eyes focusing on some hurried movement in front of him. He gestured forward with his hands, indicating that he wanted his section to follow behind the local, who was now acting as their guide.

Brannan and his squad moved quietly through the village streets. Once they reached a defensible position, Brennan deployed some of the scouts, armed with .50 caliber sniper weapons, to spots overlooking the village. The Afghan police began to move down the streets of the village, looking for locals to speak with.

Suddenly and without forewarning, the

Afghan police officers came under heavy fire. The scouts fired back, providing the officers with enough cover to retreat into the shadows of a hut.

Staff Sergeant Brannan grabbed the radio and called back to Battalion Headquarters at FOB Lagman. "Contact. Contact," he barked into the microphone. "Kharnay village. Enemy forces have pinned down our Afghan police in some of the houses. Contact is heavy. Over."

Back at headquarters, Lieutenant Colonel Stammer paced the floor, thinking about his next orders. Experience had shown that the enemy preferred to slip away before they could be challenged. This was a fleeting chance for the Americans to actually engage the enemy. "Maintain contact. *Do not let them get away*," Stammer instructed.

Brannan and his squad took the order to heart. What they could not have known was that they were seriously outnumbered: approximately 10 to 1. His squad engaged the enemy, pinning them down for several hours.

Eventually, the insurgents began to fire rocket-propelled grenades (RPGs) at their position. Brannan instructed most of his scouts to continue firing on the enemy to maintain pressure. Then he climbed into a vehicle with a few of the soldiers to try and work behind the insurgents through another village.

Almost immediately, the vehicle was struck. It took three RPG rounds and the fuel cans blew, gradually engulfing the vehicle in flames. This was a heavy loss for the Americans, for it held sensitive equipment including the patrol's only long-range satellite radio.

Brannan hurried back to his squad with shouts of encouragement. It would be two and a half hours before reinforcements would arrive by Chinook helicopters from Qalat to relieve them. Until then, their only help was air support provided by attack helicopters and the air force's ground attack aircraft. But even when confronted with air cover, the enemy continued to pound

Brannan's position. After more than two chaotic hours, helicopters brought in much-needed relief troops—60 soldiers from Chosen Company and the battalion's assault command post.

Heavy fire continued throughout the day, and the skirmish developed into a battle in its own right. A second wave of U.S. soldiers arrived, this time originating from FOB Lagman itself. This new group of soldiers from Chosen Company was charged with clearing enemy fighters from the village, but they managed to do this only after several intense firefights in an orchard against what proved to be 30 dug-in enemy fighters and additional hostile fire originating in the hills.

By the end of the day, the U.S. forces were victorious. Stammer credited aggressive tactics by Chosen Company and effective close air support and attack aviation. In particular, machine gun squad leader Staff Sergeant Mathew Blaskowski led a crucial fight on the ground with air support; Sergeant Christopher Choay led a second critical attack. Blaskowski led a gun team up a hill, engaged the enemy, and repelled several attacks, being shot in the leg in the process. Sergeant Choay led his squad to kill 13 of the enemy in an intense hour-long firefight in the orchard, eight of whom he took down himself. By the end of the day, Chosen Company and air support had killed 37 enemy fighters and captured 11. In all probability, a further one to two dozen enemy escaped, which suggests the original enemy strength was upwards of 70 in number. For their actions that day, Staff Sergeant Brannan, Staff Sergeant Blaskowski, and Sergeant Choay received Silver Star medals.

CHAPTER 7

Current Conditions and Key Players

Now that a functional government exists in Afghanistan, three groups remain that actively seek to disrupt and destabilize the new Afghan government and coalition forces. These three groups are the remnants of the Taliban, al-Qaeda, and Gulbuddin Hekmatyar's group—the Hizb-I Islami Gulbuddin (HIG).

Taliban remnants

The Taliban are the weakest and least significant of the three remaining groups. Most of its forces surrendered to Northern Alliance commanders during the initial military offensive against the Taliban regime in 2001, and many of its fighters have now switched allegiance. Between several hundred and several thousand Taliban probably remain at large in the mountains.

Forced to abandon the cities where it had first drawn the bulk of its support, the Taliban is ill equipped to wage a terrorist campaign. But these fighters are learning. The Taliban is responsible for a growing number of roadside bombings, suicide bombings, and similar attacks intended to destabilize the Afghan government and the police force, terrorize the populace, and generate injuries and casualties among military forces stationed in the country.

Al-Qaeda

Al-Qaeda is not an indigenous Afghan group.

Foreign volunteers, primarily Arabian, make up its numbers and dominate its hierarchy, as is exemplified by bin Laden. There was always a degree of tension between al-Qaeda outsiders and most Afghan people.

Pragmatism and give-and-take is traditional in Afghan politics, and these qualities have grown out of tribal relations. In traditional tribal politics, tribal elders calculate what they believe the benefit is of collaborating with another tribal group. These elders have been raised in a traditional society and are thus cautious and mistrustful of outsiders. And while the competition between rival factions in Afghanistan has often been fierce and even bloody, establishing partnerships has been pragmatic and not based on religious fanaticism. If it becomes apparent that one faction will likely emerge the winner, tribes and clans will shift their allegiance to align themselves with that party rather than fight to the death. This pattern was evident during Operation Enduring Freedom itself: few battles fought during the campaign entailed fighting to the death. Local factions transferred their allegiance from the Taliban to the Northern Alliance when it became clear who would dominate.

The members of a fanatic and extremist movement such as al-Qaeda, in contrast, have no motivation to be flexible and adaptive. As outsiders, they do not have long-term commitments to the local tribes. As fanatics motivated by an extreme anti-Western and anti-modern world view, al-Qaeda fighters are uninterested in compromise and have no reason to align themselves with the new Afghan government.

Most al-Qaeda fighters appear to have left the country in late 2001 and early 2002 in the wake of the Tora Bora fighting, as did bin Laden. Since that time, al-Qaeda has not operated in strength or as an openly armed group within Afghanistan; this is due in part to the fact that as foreigners they cannot easily hide among the native population. Instead, al-Qaeda has mounted terrorist attacks against the international forces in Afghanistan in an effort to drive coalition forces from the country and to destabilize the country.

Hizb-I Islami Gulbuddin

Perhaps the most significant insurgent group at present is Gulbuddin Hekmatyar's HIG. Unlike al-Qaeda, the HIG is a native Afghan group, at home in the country and able to move and hide among the people. Unlike the Taliban, it has a history of insurgent activities and is better adapted to sustain itself as a guerrilla movement in the mountains.

Gulbuddin Hekmatyar remains a spoiler in the convoluted world of Afghan power politics. As he did during the post-Soviet Rabbani government, he has retreated to the hills with his troops and has set off an insurgency campaign against the Kabul government.

Other challenges

Not all of Afghanistan's ills are strictly military;

the country faces the formidable problem of a devastated infrastructure. Decades of war have destroyed many roads, bridges, and municipal services. Rebuilding will be the work of a generation, even with a significant supply of outside aid. It's also worth noting that little local infrastructure existed even before the fighting of the last few years.

As well, the country is impoverished and has no substantial natural resources that can easily be tapped. Indeed, the country's sole marketable natural resource is the poppy, the seeds of which are used in opium production. Afghanistan produces more than two-thirds of the world's opium supply. Predictably, the illicit nature of the drug trade cultivates the challenges that accompany criminal activities.

Government strategy

Confronted with these very considerable challenges, Hamid Karzai's government has adopted an approach to development and change that will build gradually and that is based upon several components operating simultaneously. First of all, a new Afghan National Army (ANA) is being organized from the ground up. This force has, to a great extent, drawn upon existing Northern Alliance forces; the aim, however, is to create a completely new force that is free of the complex tangle of loyalties woven throughout the militias of the provincial warlords and the traditional tribal networks.

President Karzai's original goal was to form an army of 70,000 men by 2009. Reflecting Karzai's gradual approach, the ANA began in Kabul itself. Outside the capital, the only Afghan armed forces were the traditional militias of the Northern Alliance and the local warlords who had joined the Northern Alliance during the fighting. Karzai's strategy was to build the ANA as a force loyal to the central government in Kabul and not to regional warlords. As the ANA has grown, it has stationed units in cities across the country. The long-term objective is to supplant all regional militias with ANA troops, so that Afghanistan will have one regular, centrally controlled military force.

The new ANA got off to a slow start. It was originally envisioned that the ANA would be trained and supported by the International Security Assistance Force. However, when it came time to begin this training, ISAF resources were fully engaged with securing the Kabul area, and little progress was made. Consequently, it was decided to create a parallel but separate training program in 2003. The United States, Britain, Canada, and France deployed teams of army instructors to Kabul to train the new Afghan units.

The ANA began modestly. Three *kandaks*, or regiments, were formed within Kabul. Each kandak consisted of about 600 men. Under U.S., British, and Canadian tutelage, the ANA's kandaks slowly developed into an effective fighting and security force. In the meantime, the traditional militias that made up the Northern Alliance continued to serve as the nation's armed forces.

Members of the allied coalition in Afghanistan have undertaken different responsibilities in the creation of the ANA. The basic training of individual soldiers is conducted according to rank: the United States trains the enlisted ranks, Britain trains non-commissioned officers, and France trains the officers. Upon graduation, soldiers are divided into kandaks and sent to the Canadian-run Afghan National Training Center where they undergo collective training in groups as platoons, companies, and battalions.

By January 2003, just over 1,700 soldiers in five kandaks had completed the 10-week training course; by June of that year, 4,000 troops had been trained. At the outset, recruiting problems occurred as a result of inconsistent international support and a lack of cooperation from regional warlords. The problem of desertion also dogged the force in its early days; in the summer of 2003, the desertion rate was estimated to be 10 percent, and in mid-March 2004, estimates suggested a total of 3,000 soldiers had deserted.

Nevertheless, the ANA continued to grow and comprised 5,000 trained soldiers by July of 2003. That month, approximately 1,000 ANA soldiers were deployed in the U.S.-led Operation Warrior Sweep, the first major combat operation for Afghan troops. In 2004, the ANA reached a strength of 10,000, and in 2005, total manpower exceeded 20,000 soldiers in 30 kandaks.

Afghanistan's kandaks are now organized into five corps that are spread across the country's regions. The four corps that operate outside Kabul are each made up of five kandaks of 600 men apiece; the remaining 10 kandaks are concentrated in the Kabul Corps.

The organization of coalition forces

The organization of U.S. and international forces in Afghanistan has been complex and has, appropriately, changed over time.

During the initial phases of Operation Enduring Freedom, all U.S. forces engaged in Afghanistan were organized under the U.S.

Central Command, otherwise known as CENT-COM. Allies, particularly Britain, contributed armed forces that were integrated with CENT-COM in an exercise of direct military cooperation between the U.S. and allied nations.

As the new Afghan government was established in January 2002, circumstances became more complicated. U.S. operations in Afghanistan were ongoing, as the hunt for Taliban and al-Qaeda remnants, not to mention bin Laden himself, continued. The interim Afghan administration of Hamid Karzai cooperated fully with this U.S.-led coalition.

After its initial success stabilizing Kabul, the ISAF began to look for ways to build upon that accomplishment. They planned to branch out by creating small forward bases within the other major Afghan cities. This process grew out of work originally done by the U.S.-led coalition under Operation Enduring Freedom. Regional teams were established to support sweep and raid operations, most of which were conducted by airmobile or Special Forces troops. These out-posts became known as Joint Regional Teams.

Originally, the military objectives of Joint Regional Teams were strictly offensive in nature. Eventually, however, their mission was expand-ed into forward bases that could bring general security to outlying regions. They would then serve as centers from which international re-building efforts could be launched. Eventually, this practice evolved into what are now known as Provincial Reconstruction Teams, or PRTs.

As both ISAF and U.S.-led operations in Af-ghanistan matured and became more complex, it became evident that the efforts of the two forc-es had to be coordinated. In late 2003, the U.S. created Coalition Forces Command–Afghani-stan, or CFC–A as it was known, to achieve this end. Adjacent to ISAF headquarters, the CFC–A was headquartered in Kabul and reported to U.S. CENTCOM. This organizational structure brings all U.S. and allied "offensive" operations in Afghanistan under one organization and

CENTCOM (CENTRAL COMMAND)

All U.S. military operations are organized within a framework that divides the globe into "combatant commands." A four-star general commands each region, reporting directly to the U.S. Secretary of Defense; each general is responsible for operations that lie within his respective region. Most of the Middle East, parts of Africa, and parts of Central Asia are the responsibility of Central Command, which is headquartered at MacDill Air Force Base in Tampa, Florida. The famous General Schwarzkopf was commander of CENTCOM during the first Gulf War. General Tommy Franks was commander of CENTCOM from July 2000 until July 2003, when General John Abizaid took over.

facilitates close cooperation between parties. Both headquarters now oversee their respective operations across Afghanistan: the CFC-A concentrates offensive efforts on tracking and eradicating remaining terrorists and insurgents, while the ISAF focus is defensive security. A U.S. officer always oversees CFC-A, although other nations contribute forces in direct cooperation with the U.S. ISAF is always under the command of a NATO officer who, it is agreed, is not a U.S. officer.

As of early 2006, CFC-A deployed 18,000 U.S. and 3,000 coalition personnel from 20 nations. ISAF forces numbered approximately 8,000, and it was expanding throughout the country. Control of a second multinational brigade in Kandahar is being transferred from CFC-A to ISAF.

Disarmament, Demobilization, and Reintegration: the second phase of stabilizing Afghanistan

The second major component of the government strategy, which complements the gradual expansion of the ANA, is the international program for "Disarmament, Demobilization, and Reintegration," known as the DDR program. This coalition-sponsored program sees regional militias disarmed, their soldiers demobilized, and the men in question reintegrated into civilian life.

The DDR program is run by the UN Assistance Mission in Afghanistan (UNAMA), and features a broadly integrated approach to the problem. The emphasis is not just on collecting weapons but also on the humans who carry them. The former factional fighters are identified, separated from their previous armed groups, returned to their traditional family homes, and then sponsored through a special program to reintegrate them into civilian life. It is the last—and critical—step in particular that makes the DDR program so unique. While not without its challenges, this approach has been remarkably effective.

While the HIG, the Taliban remnants, and some al-Qaeda agents have contested the new Afghan government's control of the country, the chief threat has not been insurgents. Rather, the principal challenge to stability is the nation's warlords—each one protective of his own power base, prestige, and position. It was, of course, this very warlord rivalry that led to the ruinous civil war following the Soviet withdrawal.

How can the Karzai government in Kabul avoid the fate of the Rabbani government that came before it? There were substantial fears in 2003 that the country's future would follow a similar course. As many analysts and commentators pointed out, this was the established pattern in Afghanistan.

And the Karzai government's position did seem tenuous. It was propped up by ISAF, whose operations were confined to Kabul. The new army had merely three battalions of soldiers. Most importantly, the country was still home to the culture, practices, and prerogatives of warlords and their militias. Those same warlords were members of the Northern Alliance and now, quite likely, ministers in the new government; however, their power flowed from their militias, which were in essence private armies. While armed militias in Afghanistan had always been loyal to their tribal leaders, so too were contemporary militias loyal to individuals, not the state. The fact of the matter was that Karzai, the elected head-of-state, controlled one of the smallest armed forces in the country.

To deal with this situation, Karzai adopted a canny strategy. His plan was to strengthen the power of the central government incrementally, and thereby not rattle the existing delicate balance of power on the one hand nor leave the central government weak and necessarily passive on the other. To accomplish this, Karzai's strategy was to gradually reduce the militias, while simultaneously strengthening the central government's forces. A key tool in this strategy has been the internationally backed Disarmament, Demobilization, and Reintegration program, which can be deployed in a targeted way to weaken and disband private militias. International officials in Kabul often use *DDR* as a verb: "to DDR" a warlord means to use the DDR process to cancel out the strength—and thereby the threat to stability—that a warlord's private army represents.

The success of the DDR program and the stability of the country then relies, to some extent, on positioning new ANA kandaks to fill the void, and sometimes this means hiring the soldiers that were just demobilized.

The final stratagem in the DDR process is lateral promotion. Karzai has been quick to offer the DDR'ed, and now unoccupied, warlords government positions in Kabul.

DDR STATISTICS (AS OF NOVEMBER 2005)

Number of small arms collected: **36,571**

Number of heavy weapons collected: **11,004**

Number of troops disarmed: **63,380**

Number of troops demobilized: **62,044**

Number of troops reintegrated: **60,646**

The situation in Herat in the summer and fall of 2004 was a test case for this strategy. Ismail Kahn was a popular but recalcitrant warlord. While he served as a prominent Northern Alliance commander in the final campaign, he enjoyed a significant local power base after the war. Ismail Kahn was a particularly independent warlord; he controlled a surprisingly healthy cross-border trade between the Herat area and Iran, which generated significant revenue independent of Kabul's central control.

Over time, Ismail Kahn's militia was incrementally DDR'ed—to the extent that they were unable to offer serious resistance when Kabul ordered two new ANA kandaks into the area. The ANA's arrival did provoke a small confrontation, but the national army forces were able to convince the local militia to back off. Khan was subsequently offered the position of government minister of mines and industry in Kabul.

The success of this initial DDR effort convinced Karzai that he could use the same strategy elsewhere. A similar process was exercised with Fahim Kahn's militia in Kabul and eventually neutralized a sizable coercive force in the capital. Fahim Kahn had been the second in command after Ahmed Massoud in the Northern Alliance; when Massoud was assassinated, Fahim Kahn succeeded him, to become the overall military commander in the campaign that deposed the Taliban. After the war, he became the new regime's first minister of defense and one of the key powerbrokers upon which Karzai came to depend. Once Fahim Kahn's militia was DDR'ed and absorbed by the new ANA, Karzai eased him out of his minister of defense role, though he was pacified with the title "marshal for life" of the Afghan National Army.

There has been a slight increase in insurgent activity in Afghanistan in 2006, particularly in and around Kandahar. This appears to be a renewed effort by the Taliban to assert its presence. Significantly, however, the Taliban has altered its tactics from conventional efforts that aim to capture territory to hit-and-run terrorist-style attacks. This change doubtless reflects the Taliban's weakened strength. In response, the international coalition appears to be stepping up its offensive patrolling.

CHAPTER 8

The Future of Afghanistan

There are solid grounds for cautious optimism about the future of Afghanistan. One might considered this rather astounding, given the long and tumultuous history of the country, evident in the remains of the many empires that litter its mountain passes and the murderous infighting that has plagued Afghanistan for so much of its history. These difficulties and this history should not be discounted: their traces remain deeply ingrained characteristics of the country. Nevertheless, in light of the progress made toward stable government, the disarmament of private militias that has occurred since Hamid Karzai was appointed interim leader, and the momentum that has been gained, foundations have been established on which hope can be built. They have already improved immeasurably since the Taliban was chased out of Afghanistan.

Afghanistan: the worst case

Despite the tremendous and hopeful changes that have occurred in Afghanistan since the Taliban regime was forced to flee Kabul at the end of 2001, it is not difficult to imagine a worst-case scenario for Afghanistan's future. Indeed, for years, imagining such a worst-case outcome was the stock in trade of most analysts of and commentators on the region. Several substantial and threatening problems still bedevil the country, any one or combination of which could serve to derail the engine of Afghanistan's newfound path and stability. The following list of challenges pose the greatest threats.

Warlordism. A return to fractious civil war is perhaps the worst fear. Certainly, Afghanistan's history demonstrates it is inclined this way. President Karzai's precarious political balancing act could fail, and the delicate consensus upon which the central government is built could collapse. Outlying regions of the country are still dominated by local strongmen, and they could once again organize private or tribal militias to deal with squabbles amongst themselves. The Rabbani government collapsed as a consequence of tribal feuding, and it is not yet certain the Karzai government can withstand these same forces should they emerge again.

Insurgency and economic collapse. Al-Qaeda and the Taliban are concentrating their efforts on creating unrest via terrorist attacks. Their efforts aim to sow fear amongst the populace and thereby generate a loss of faith in the ability of the new government to stabilize the political, economic, and military elements of the country. The recent surge in terrorist-style attacks is almost certainly an attempt by the Taliban to implement this strategy. However, this strategy of weakness appears to be alienating the local populace.

With respect to economics and infrastructure, Afghanistan is still a devastated country in which poverty and unemployment are rife. This can generate various social ills, instability, and unrest. Al-Qaeda and the Taliban have thus sought to undermine the country's economic development. They have done this, specifically, by targeting international relief organizations and new generators of economic strength.

International abandonment. A principal fear of the Karzai government is that the international community will lose interest in Afghanistan and depart before stabilization and reconstruction are complete. Following the Soviet withdrawal from Afghanistan in 1989, the concerns of the country were for the most part forgotten and ignored by the outside world—a disinterest that created the social and economic vacuum that made possible the rise of the Taliban.

Drug trafficking. Organized crime engaged in large-scale drug production and smuggling can effectively destabilize a country, as Colombia demonstrates. Afghanistan's precarious economic and social condition, paired with the absence of sound social or legal infrastructures and the reality of precarious agricultural resources, makes the rise and influence of organized crime a threat that cannot be discounted.

None of these trends, obstacles, and threats is mutually exclusive. In the worst-case scenario, some or all of these elements could combine to frustrate and reverse the conditional progress that has been made under the Karzai Government and sponsorship of the international community. This could cause the country to spiral back into the social, economic, and military chaos of a failed state. Drug trafficking could undermine the forces of law and order, particularly in combination with the practices of a terrorist insurgency. This could hamstring economic development, keeping the country poor and restive and populated in part with many unemployed young men hungry to find purpose, direction, and financial security. Confronted with this intractable set of conditions, it is not inconceivable that the international community would tire of the military and economic drain this circumstance represents and withdraw its aid, organizations, and military support. Paradoxically, this would prove a greater possibility if bin Laden were to be captured, which might lead some in the West to conclude that its mission in Afghanistan was complete. Without the stabilizing presence of international contributors, a return to rampant warlordism might not be far behind.

Afghanistan: the best case

Fortunately, as a result of the productive and constructive social and military changes that have taken root in Afghanistan since the end of Operation Enduring Freedom, it is not difficult to imagine a positive future for this growing nation. Many signs point to a more hopeful future, and both the new Afghan government of Hamid Karzai and the support and contributions of the international community indicate some promising potential in the future.

Continued DDR. The Disarmament, Demobilization, and Reintegration program undertaken in Afghanistan is truly historic. The disarmament of formerly warring factions has been attempted many times in Afghanistan's history, with uneven results. The current disarmament program in Afghanistan has been more successful than most, but there are still plenty of weapons available to any faction that wants them. What makes the DDR process in Afghanistan unique is the integrated approach it has taken with respect to the *R* component in this process—reintegrating militants from all factions into civil society. The bottom line is that the country is now less an armed camp divided between rival factions than it was previously, and the DDR process has significantly reduced the prevalence of armed militias that exist beyond the control of the central government.

Growth of the Afghan National Army. The development of a strong and loyal military force controlled by the national government is one factor that is powerfully linked with the establishment of effective, stable governments throughout history. This has been true since the Roman Empire. The development of the ANA, shaped from the ground up by the Afghan government, has produced a competent military force dedicated to the central government and not disparate militias loyal to a cadre of warlords.

Economic growth. There are signs of life from the Afghan economy. Generous development programs are underway. The numbers of unemployed and underemployed are slowly falling. There are hopeful signs that these trends will continue.

Stabilization efforts. The active presence of international military operations that continue to hunt down remaining insurgent elements in Afghanistan have met with considerable success. The Taliban, the HIG, and al-Qaeda cannot continue to wage a losing military effort indefinitely. Insurgencies, as history shows, have the capacity to continue for decades or longer, but Afghanistan's insurgents need not be completely pacified in order for the government or the nation to succeed. Instead, the insurgent forces must be reined in sufficiently to enable the growth of political, social, and economic forces that will in turn stabilize the Afghan government and enable it to master its internal security. This goal appears to be within sight.

Democratization. Finally, it must be observed that democracy appears to be taking root in Afghanistan. The new constitution, while not without some disagreement among the many varied political and religious groups, outlines the means to sustain and develop the democratic rule of law. The constitution appears, as well, to have the endorsement of the people, who actively participated in the voting process of the nation's first democratic elections.

In light of these positive developments, Afghanistan appears to be on the road to a real recovery. While it is simple, and sometimes tempting, to make pessimistic predictions about systems or situations in the midst of momentous changes—a longstanding practice of news media pundits—such negative assessments are not always accurate or responsible. Most commentators, for example, once evaluated the circumstances of Bosnia as hopeless; it is now a region of relative peace. Previously relentless civil wars and insurgencies can end. Afghanistan remains poor and must confront a range of social and economic obstacles, but if it is able to maintain its momentum toward military and political stability and legitimacy, it appears to be on the road to becoming a newly peaceful developing nation.

It should also be remembered that a remarkable military campaign, one that deposed the restrictive Taliban regime, made this hopeful scenario possible. Operation Enduring Freedom, it appears, was not launched in vain and has created these rewarding conditions.

A Timeline of Al-Qaeda Attacks

February 23, 1993

First World Trade Center bombing. A truck bomb in the Center's parking garage kills six and injures hundreds but fails to cause significant structural damage.

June 25, 1996

Khobar Towers bombing. A truck bomb kills 19 U.S. servicemen and injures many others in Dhahran, Saudi Arabia.

August 7, 1998

U.S. embassy bombings. Truck bombs destroy the U.S. embassies in Nairobi, Kenya, and Dar es Salaam, Tanzania, killing 234 (12 of whom were Americans), and injuring more than 5,000.

October 5, 2000

U.S.S. *Cole* bombing. Suicide bombers piloting a small rubber boat blast a hole in the U.S.S. *Cole* while the ship is docked in Aden, Yemen, killing 17 sailors and wounding 39.

September 11, 2001

Hijacked aircraft attack and destroy the World Trade Center and severely damage the Pentagon with great loss of life.

Note

Following the loss of their camps in Afghanistan, capture of many of their leaders of the second and third ranks, and the disruption of their organization, it does not appear as if al-Qaeda itself has mounted any terrorist attacks since 9/11. However, sympathetic Muslim extremist groups inspired by and linked to al-Qaeda have mounted various attacks from the Bali bombing of October 2002 to the July 2005 London bombings.

Chronology of Messages from Osama bin Laden*

October 7, 2001
(filmed in late September/early October)
A threatening tape is released at the commencement of the U.S. attacks on Afghanistan and shown on Aljazeera. Also on tape are bin Laden spokesman Abu Ghaith, chief lieutenant Ayman al Zawahiri, and Mohammed Atef, bin Laden's military commander.

November 3, 2001
(filmed in late October/early November)
Bin Laden, dressed in camouflage and armed with an AK-47, says in a tape aired by Aljazeera that the war in Afghanistan is a religious war: "The people of Afghanistan had nothing to do with this matter. The campaign, however, continues to unjustly annihilate the villagers and civilians, children, women, and innocent people."

* Unless otherwise noted, the recordings were taped at roughly the same time as their broadcast dates.

December 27, 2001
(taped mid-November 2001)

Dubbed the "Gaunt Tape"—so called because bin Laden appears haggard and doesn't move his left arm—this item is thought to have been recorded around November 19, 2001. In the tape, bin Laden refers to the U.S. bombing of a mosque in Khost "several days" earlier. The U.S. bombed a mosque in Khost on November 16.

April 17–18, 2002
(taped in October 2001)

The "Riverside tape," believed filmed in October 2001, is shown on Arabic-language broadcasters MBC and Aljazeera in slightly different versions. In this tape, bin Laden praises the impact the September 11 attacks had on the U.S. economy.

November 12, 2002

In a statement carried on Aljazeera, bin Laden calls President George W. Bush the "pharaoh of this age," and lists recent attacks made against Westerners. Specifically, he notes, "The incidents that have taken place since the raids on New York and Washington up until now—like the killing of Germans in Tunisia and the French in Karachi, the bombing of the giant French tanker in Yemen, the killing of marines in Kuwait and the British and Australians in the Bali explosions, the recent

operation in Moscow, and some sporadic operations here and there—are only reactions and
reciprocal actions." It is the first bin Laden
message in nearly a year that can be dated
with reasonable accuracy.

February 11, 2003

Bin Laden criticizes U.S. plans for war against
Iraq, citing Baghdad's historical role as a capital
of Islam. In the statement, carried on Aljazeera,
bin Laden asserts, "We are following up with
great interest and extreme concern the crusaders'
preparations for war to occupy a former capital
of Islam."

February 16, 2003

Entitled "Bin Laden's Sermon for the Feast of the
Sacrifice," the statement broadcast on Aljazeera
criticizes President George W. Bush and British
Prime Minister Tony Blair for planning the war on
Iraq. In it, bin Laden asserts that Western plans
to interfere with Islamic nations do not end with
Iraq: "The preparations underway at present for
an attack upon Iraq are but one link in a chain of
attacks—[currently] in preparation—on the countries of the region, including Syria, Iran, Egypt,
and Sudan."

April 8, 2003

On the eve of the U.S. capture of Baghdad, bin Laden urges suicide attacks and calls on Muslims to rise up against Arab governments that support the U.S.-led attack on Iraq.

September 10, 2003
(most likely filmed in 2001)

Aljazeera airs a combined audio and videotape showing bin Laden walking down a mountain path with Ayman al Zawahiri, his chief lieutenant. U.S. officials noted that the audio made no reference to current events, while Zawahiri did, leading them to believe Zawahiri's comments were recent and that bin Laden's had been recorded at some point in the past.

October 18, 2003

Aljazeera broadcasts two audiotapes said to be made by Osama bin Laden, vowing more suicide attacks inside and outside the United States and demanding the United States withdraw from Iraq. "We, God willing," the voice warns, "will continue to fight you and will continue martyrdom operations."

January 4, 2004
The al-Qaeda leader remarks on audio tape that Muslim and Arab leaders were jolted by Saddam's ouster because foreign forces could topple dictatorial regimes.

April 15, 2004
In an audiotape message, bin Laden offers a truce to European countries if they leave the Middle East within 90 days; if they don't, he threatens they will become the targets of al-Qaeda attacks.

October 29, 2004
On videotape broadcast on Aljazeera, bin Laden warns Americans, "Your security is not in the hands of Kerry or Bush or al-Qaeda. Your security is in your own hands." He also claims full responsibility for the September 11, 2001, attacks in the United States.

January 19, 2006
In an audio tape with no video, which U.S. officials believe to be genuine, bin Laden attacked President Bush and offered a "truce" with the West if it withdraws all troops from the Middle East.

Afghanistan by the Numbers

SECURITY	
70,000	U.S. goal for trained Afghan National Army Soldiers
31,000	Soldiers trained for the Afghan National Army (through June 2005)
18,000	U.S. troops in Afghanistan as of February 2006
147,000	U.S. troops in Iraq as of February 2006
2,300	Canadian troops in Afghanistan as of February 2006
1	Estimated billions of dollars spent per month on U.S. military operations in Afghanistan
1,800	Estimated number of warlords in Afghanistan who still maintain private militias

SOLDIER DEATHS

55 U.S. soldiers killed between October 2001 and December 2002

86 U.S. soldiers killed between January 2005 and October 2005

10 Canadian soldiers killed since October 2001

DRUG PRODUCTION

20,000 Estimated number of acres of poppies under cultivation, 2001

324,000 Estimated number of acres of poppies under cultivation, 2004

4,600 Tons of opium produced in Afghanistan, 2004

HUMAN INDICATORS

43 Afghani life expectancy, 2005 estimate

70 Percent of Afghanis who suffer from malnutrition

13 Percent of Afghanis with reliable access to clean water

56 Percent of Afghanis living below the UN-defined poverty line

Select Bibliography and Recommended Reading

No comprehensive military history of the U.S.-led invasion of Afghanistan has been written. There are, however, many books that recount the earlier history of Afghanistan, from ancient times to the rise of the Taliban regime: Christopher Andrew and Vasili Mitrokhin, *The Sword and the Shield: The Mitrokhin Archive and the Secret History of the KGB* (Basic Books, 1999); Lester W. Grau, *The Soviet-Afghan War: How a Super Power Fought and Lost* (University Press of Kansas, 2002); John C. Griffiths, *Afghanistan: Key to a Continent* (Andre Deutsch, 1981); Jon Lee Anderson, *The Lion's Grave: Dispatches from Afghanistan* (Grove Press, 2002); Kurt Lohbeck, introduction by Dan Rather, *Holy War, Unholy Victory: Eyewitness to the CIA's Secret War in Afghanistan* (Regnery Publishing, 1993); Sean M. Maloney, "Afghanistan Four Years On: An Assess-